GREATER
EXPECTATIONS

ALI CARTER

books

"Greater Expectations serves as a compelling illustration of the transformative potential that coaching and goal-setting can bring to both a business and its owner. This book is a powerful, engaging, and motivational read. Ali's honest and witty account of his journey, starting from scratch and navigating through the challenges, is refreshingly candid. I am thrilled that ActionCOACH played a pivotal role in contributing to his success."

Brad Sugars, Chairman & Founder of ActionCOACH

Best wishes for finding your future.

Ali.

Published in 2023 by YAKKA Books

ISBN Paperback : 978-1-7395550-0-9
Ebook : 978-1-7395550-1-6

Published with the help of Indie Authors World
www.indieauthorsworld.com

Do you want to start making a positive change to your life straight away?

One of my personal goals is to help people, just like you, improve the quality of their lives. You can download the goal-setting exercise, detailed in this book, for free.

If you want to start taking giant steps to a wealthier and happier life, visit greaterexpectations.life and download the free goal-setting and manifesting exercise sheet.

It's my gift to you, as you start your journey. Good Luck!

GREATER
EXPECTATIONS

ACKNOWLEDGEMENTS

To:

Bailey, Amelia, Dempsey & Dexter

It's all for you. It has always been, all for you

Caroline

My sister, best-friend and cheerleader

Ian, Belinda, Jess, Danielle, 'The Dream Team' and all our mediators at Mediate UK

I cannot thank you enough

Simon at ActionCOACH

Thank you for showing me the way. And cheering my every step

Willie, JB, Maria, Phil, Adrian, Geoff, Nick, Rowland, Rowan, Matt, Aiden, Tony, Keith, Felix, Sam, Andy, Pumba, Di, Sophie, Alan, Jacko, Jeff, Mischa, Lyndon, David, Will, James, Kane, Robbie, all my family and my amazing family in-law (especially Becky for her editing help!)

Thank you - you all played an important part in showing kindness and friendship to me

To Amber

I wouldn't be here if it wasn't for you - I adore you

To Mum

Sleep peacefully. I am so grateful for all you did for me

Health Warning:

Some of the themes in this book may make difficult reading and could trigger painful memories for the reader.

There are also adult themes and a fair amount of swearing. (Do not read if easily offended).

Definitely do not read, if you don't want to make any radical changes to your life and improve it significantly.

Here goes ...

PROLOGUE

Tuesday 9th April 2019, approximately 8pm

The Travelodge Bracknell is a particularly depressing grey concrete building. Favoured by workmen staying overnight on various building projects, the car park is full of white vans and work trucks. If you are lucky enough to find a parking space in between two such vehicles, you are unlikely to be able to open either the driver or passenger door successfully, so you can sometimes find yourself exiting your vehicle through the boot.

As you enter the foyer there is the standard unhealthy snack vending machine on your left, with the equally standard 'Out of Order' sign taped to it. Check-in is super-efficient, however, and you can be in your room and looking out at the gloomy view of the A329 within three minutes of leaving your car boot.

There are two Travelodges in Bracknell (I'm not sure what the collective noun is for a Travelodge - a despondency of Traveli perhaps?) and this is, unbelievably, the nicer of the two. If you weren't depressed before you arrived here, there is a good chance you will be by the time you leave.

But I was depressed. Deeply, emotionally and dangerously depressed. The pillars supporting me and carrying me through the past few years had either been eroded away or deliberately destroyed by myself. The business I had spent eight years trying to turn into something worthwhile, something to make me feel relevant in the world and something to support my family, was about to collapse.

The mistakes I had made up to this point in the business were all conspiring to attack me at the same time. And my wife and children ... my poor, beautiful, long-suffering wife, who had supported me and believed in me through all these years ... both she and my children deserved so much better. How unfortunate for them, how unlucky that they had allowed me into their lives. I had let them down in the most terrible of ways. I had failed them all.

In my depressed mind, the trade-off was a simple one. A great, once in a lifetime – quite literally – bargain deal. I had now held my life insurance for the qualifying period and, if I took my own life, they would pay out a lump sum of £250,000. As the beneficiary, my wife could buy a small house. She could perhaps treat the children to a holiday and give herself an opportunity to find someone who wouldn't let them all down as badly as I felt I had done. Someone who wasn't such a loser. Someone who was supposed to be here on the earth. Someone not as fucked-up as me. My warped and tired brain saw it as a fantastic business opportunity. Nothing more. It made perfect sense.

I had chosen a nice bottle of white wine. A Marlborough Sauvignon Blanc from New Zealand – the good stuff. I looked at the pills I had emptied out over the bed. Paracetamol, ibuprofen (the super strong 500mg ones), co-codamol, some I wasn't even sure what they were for, and some diamond-shaped pills we shall come on to later. I grabbed a handful of pills and shoved them in my mouth, like the fat kid from *Charlie and the Chocolate Factory* drinking from the chocolate river. The taste as they started to dissolve on my tongue was dry and bitter so I took a large swig from the cheap plastic glass of expensive Sauvignon-Blanc. It happily washed them all down.

I started crying. Uncontrollable tears. Flooding down my face. My shoulders were arching forwards in convulsions as I thought of how many people in my life had come to realise what a terrible person I was and had (quite rightly in my mind) rejected me. My friends, my father, my 'real' father, even my beautiful daughter. I grabbed another handful of pills, not even looking at them. It was like scooping up a handful of M&M's at a kid's birthday party. I shoved them into my mouth and refilled the flimsy plastic cup with wine. This time I downed it in one.

I wasn't sure how many pills I had swallowed by this time, and it occurred to me that I was not sure how many I would need to put me permanently to sleep and successfully claim my insurance money. *I know*, I thought. *I'll Google it.* Grabbing my laptop, I opened the browser and saw I had the little red notification on my Facebook page. It could be someone selling something in my area, or someone posting something about their 'amazing life' … I clicked on it. Because 'brain law' says you have to click on something when there is a little red dot next to it, right?

A friend had just written a post about how much they missed their father, who had recently passed away. That particular friend had managed to build up a successful business. They had a gorgeous house with gorgeous children in a gorgeous area of

Surrey. *I'll never get close to achieving what they have done,* I thought. *I'm such a fucking loser.*

I drank some more wine and picked up a few more of the pills from the bed, absent-mindedly liking this friend's post, while continuing to pop the pills into my mouth. In my distorted mind, I was absolutely certain that these friends would never want anything to do with me again. I was convinced, in my depressed state, that all my friends held regular updates to collate information about me and then rigorously slag me off.

Over the next hour, I sat in my plastic desk chair, stalking various people on Facebook. It was the day before my wedding anniversary: eight years. But I wasn't going to be able to celebrate with my wife, because I was away in a Travelodge in Bracknell, trying to save my business and trying to help my mother – who was now showing the clear signs of Alzheimer's that she had been telling us about for a year. Well, in my opinion, my wife was about to get the best anniversary present ever. A quarter-of-a-million-pound-cheque and the chance to finally live the half decent, happy life that she so deserved.

There were about a dozen pills left on the bed. I am not sure how many I had taken already, but I reckoned one final push could see me through. And then something stopped me for a moment. I have no idea what. I paused and, through my tears, I turned back around to my laptop and messaged someone I vaguely knew from my rugby club days.

Hi Emma,
We don't know each other that well, but can I ask ... what do you think about me? (and don't worry I am not cracking on to you!) but genuinely what do you think when you hear someone mention my name? Sorry if I come across as weird.

It must have been one of the strangest messages to receive. I anticipated the reply coming back as something similar to: *Well, me and most of the people at the rugby club think you are a complete twat and the world would be a far better place without you.*

Fortunately, Emma was awake and had read my message. She replied immediately: *I'm curious where the question is coming from, but the first things that come to mind are business, a family man and a great sense of humour.*

Emma didn't know it, but her immediate and kind response had just saved my life. Taking another final swig of the Marlborough Sauvignon-Blanc, I rushed to the melamine ensuite and shoved my fingers so far down my throat, I impulsively wanted to bite down on them to stop myself. I vomited into the toilet. A little at first and then a lot. It felt like my throat was on fire and the taste in my mouth was horrific. But I kept at it, forcing my fingers down my throat time and time again, until I could not bring anything else up. I returned to my laptop and told Emma I was struggling with 'doing life' a little bit, that I was drunk and that I would be fine.

Emma spent some time reassuring me and I bade her good night. Not knowing and, by this stage, not really caring if my vomiting would be enough to help me, I collapsed on the bed, completely physically and emotionally exhausted. I fell asleep on top of the sheets in my clothes. I knew, from seeing many dead bodies in my time as a police officer, that if I was going to die, it would be tragic enough for the poor Travelodge employee who found me, without adding the trauma of finding me naked as well.

I disintegrated into a deep sleep, with absolutely no idea whether I would wake up.

***

I woke up. I had a splitting headache, which I thought was the highest form of irony as I had taken so many bloody paracetamol. My mouth felt dryer than Ghandi's flip-flop and my throat was throbbing with pain where I had scratched the lining away with my fingers. But that was not the only thing throbbing. In my absent-mindedness I had included several Viagra pills in my medical pic 'n' mix. I looked down in trepidation. I swear the reason for the headache was not the bottle of wine I had consumed, but the fact that my body was busy pumping every available litre of blood to my genitalia.

I smiled to myself, as I joked that – had I not woken up – they would have struggled to get the lid on the coffin! I pulled myself out of bed and took off the clothes that I was still wearing from the previous day.

Damn it, I thought. *This is almost a waste of an erection. I would have been happy going in to bat for England holding this thing!*

I climbed into the shower and braced myself. The cold water hit me like I had just run face first into a glass door. I let it pelt me with freezing cold sprays, as though it was my penance for my depressive episode the prior evening. Eventually the water had its effect; my mind was clear and my penis was, finally, resting at flaccid.

I got dressed and I drove to our new office in Binfield, put a fixed but false smile on my face and carried on as though nothing had happened. I had always managed to hide my depression from others and, once again, I felt I had gotten away with it.

'You are valuable just because you exist. Not because of what you do or what you have done, but simply because you are.'

— Max Lucado

INTRODUCTION

Is your life a little bit shit? Did you expect things to be so much better than they currently are? Are you going through the drudgery of going to work every day, to support a life that is just about OK, but isn't amazing? Are you sacrificing your happiness and what you want to do, for the security of raising your family? Are you nowhere near the best version of yourself that you could be?

If you have picked up this book, chances are the answer to at least one of those questions is a resounding 'yes!'

In this book, I will explain how the best chance you have to improve your life significantly and smash through your goals, is to start or expand your own business. I will share with you the six pillars of support you need to nurture – as these will ensure you are the best version of yourself and in the optimal position to live the life you want to lead. I will also introduce you to the six business pillars that will provide the foundations you need to build a business that can fund the lifestyle you want and help you achieve your own greater expectations.

The book is in three parts. Part one will dive in to these six pillars of support before talking about my life to date. You'll come to understand why the six pillars of support are so important and how I came to realise that. You will journey with me through the events that led to the founding of my business.

I understand my back story may not be massively relevant to you but I have included it in the book, as I wanted to show you that if a slightly fucked-up, anxious and – for many years – depressed person can do it, then I hope it gives you the confidence that you can do it as well. I also wanted to explain a little about mental health and how you can help yourself and others through your own actions and mindset.

In Part Two, I take you through my journey of building up a business and how I built this up from nothing, to a multi award-winning company that is the largest and best reviewed of its kind in the UK. I show you how I finally became a leader and go through the many pitfalls I hope you can avoid.

In Part Three, we take a look at you and your own business or life decisions. I talk you through the six pillars on which your business will grow and thrive. I take you through how to actually start your own business, how to grow it and what you need to put in place to make it a success. I will explain how goal setting and manifesting play an important role in achieving a better life and show you how to do this.

There is a formula to running a business, and running your life, which, just like a difficult recipe, needs to be followed to ensure you give yourself the best chance of success. I also explain why starting or growing an existing business gives you the greatest chance at achieving a life that meets your (greater) expectations.

It is important that I stress to you now: *No one is coming for you.* There is no magical event that will occur, to change your life forever. You won't win the lottery, or find happiness once you hit a certain milestone in your life. You really need to take action now. Make changes now and become happier, now. I hope this book will give you the confidence, tools and knowledge to do so. Drop us a message via www.greaterexpectations.life to let me know how you are getting on.

'The best time to plant a tree was twenty years ago. The second best time is now.'

— Chinese proverb

PART ONE

MAKING A MESS

1

THE SIX PILLARS TO SUPPORT YOU IN YOUR LIFE

I want you to imagine that you are a square piece of wood. Yes, please, bear with me on this analogy. You want to raise yourself up from the banality of being a small square plank but, to do so, you need support. This support can take the form of six distinct pillars; the wider the pillars, the better that support, and the more stable you will be. You see where I am headed with this? You need solid and wide pillars of support to raise you up from your current level to get to where you want to be. Those pillars need to be strong to keep you there when things start to get difficult. And, at some point on your journey to a better life, they *will* get difficult. After all, if it was easy to do – we would all be successful entrepreneurs.

The six pillars of support are:

- Friends
- Family
- Relationship
- Work
- Coach or Mentor
- Religion / Higher Power / Spirituality

Let's look at each column of support in turn:

Friends

Do you have a good network of friends, who are on your side and who will give you honest feedback when you need it? Or perhaps you have a small group of friends who you know you can rely on to help you through when things get bad? Having genuine support from your friends, as you venture out to set up your own business or change your life for the better, can be vital to help you get off the ground. You want to surround yourself with people who will encourage, advise, help, support your business and talk to their friends about it. You want to avoid friends who will talk your ideas down, laugh at your ambition, get jealous of you and surround you with negativity. And there will usually be at least one friend like that. That's OK, you can simply keep away from them, ignore them or just smile and allow them to be wrong. Because you are taking massive action to improve your life – and they are likely to be stuck in the drudgery of theirs. We'll call this friend 'Nagging Nigel'.

Do you have a friend who has been successful in their own business? Or in their career? Do you have a friend who is a cheerleader for you? Who you know would drop everything if you needed help? We'll call this friend 'Supportive Sally'. You need to pay more attention to Supportive Sally and less attention to Nagging Nigel. Nigel will just bring you down and make your *Friends* column weaker. Sally will provide a great foundation.

In readiness for your new business, you ideally need to surround yourselves with people who will raise you up, not bring you down. You can search out networking groups, self-help groups and mastermind groups, where you will have people who have either gone through what you are about to do, or are on that journey themselves and you can mutually support each other. You could even download and use the YAKKA app to meet like-minded, ambitious people. Get rid of Nigel, buy Sally a present and get your *Friends* column as strong as it can be for the journey ahead.

It was during my unfortunate episode in the Bracknell Travelodge that I believed, incorrectly of course, that my *Friends* column had collapsed because of the decisions I had made in my business. Had it been just the *Friends* column that had collapsed, I would have been OK. But I also had other pillars collapsing as well.

Family

I remember my mother's look of disappointment and disbelief when I told her I was leaving the safety of a career in the police to set up my own business. Her mood changed a little for the better, when I told her I was running a rugby-themed café instead, but, nevertheless, I might as well have just told her I was going to join ISIS. She was that concerned for my future.

I shouldn't have been surprised. I had, a few years earlier, suggested to my mother that we re-mortgage on her two investment properties and buy a portfolio of properties, do them up and re-mortgage again, until she had a thriving property portfolio that I was happy to manage. She explained that the thought of having all that money owed on mortgages would keep her awake at night and the stress would be unbearable. What if someone didn't pay their rent? What if we couldn't get a tenant into one of them? What if something went wrong? No, the idea was dead before it was properly conceived.

My mother's Alzheimer's had deteriorated, to the point where she did not know me, by the time the business had become a success, whereby I could have made her proud of my decision to leave the police. But I had my sister Caroline as my cheerleader – my family version of Supportive Sally – and it would be my sister who would prove to be the one to make my family column stronger and more supportive.

Reach out to your family and explain what you are going to do and why you are going to do it. Blatantly ask for their support and help – to act as your cheerleaders and network marketers. Tell them how you need them to be with you on this journey.

The stress from my mother's Alzheimer's diagnosis, the additional help she needed, the fact her kitchen roof had crashed down that morning and needed sorting out, and the fact that she kept calling the police and accusing her friends and family, myself included, of stealing from her, weakened my *Family* column at just the time when my other pillars were weakened too. I allowed her diagnosis – something I could not control – to affect my mental health, something I *could and should* have been able to control better.

Relationship

This is such an important column of support to get right. If your partner does not support you in what you are doing, you will most likely fail. It is important to set your sights on the same goals. And this is why, when you do the goal-setting exercise that I explain in Chapter 14, you should do this with your partner, together.

If you are intending to stay with your partner for the foreseeable future, then you need to make sure that they are on your side and you are both working towards a common goal.

Your success will be their success and, if you are married, your business will be their business, irrespective of whether you are both shareholders, directors or not.

It is really important here that I clarify: you don't need to have the same goals. You don't need to both be ambitious and you don't need to both work in the business together. Indeed, if one of you has a full-time job that brings in a guaranteed income, it can help reduce the risk if your new venture fails.

By doing the goal-setting exercise together, you are aware of what drives the other person, what their dreams are and what they are already proud of achieving. It is highly likely that the majority of the goals you set will need money to help achieve them. And, if successful, your business will provide you with the income or capital that you will need to make both your dreams come true. No one else, other than perhaps your children, is likely to benefit as much from your business succeeding as your partner will. You need them on board to help get you through the days when you are down, when you are stressed up to your eyeballs, when you can't sleep or when all you want to do is sleep. You need them supporting you when you need to work on a weekend or a bank holiday, and when you can't afford to go on a family holiday for a few years because the business needs you at home.

You need them to buy into cutting costs and perhaps selling things you both enjoyed having, in order to give your business the vital oxygen (money) that it needs to get started and grow. Finally, you need them to pick you up when you fail and tell you to go back out, learn from your mistakes and do it all over again, until you find a business or methodology that *does* work.

That takes a very special type of person. And if you are lucky enough to have such a partner, you need to make sure they know that they are your most important column of support, so that they never leave.

If you don't currently have a partner, then that is easy. You just need to make sure, when you do, they are just like the person I describe above. Following the advice I give in this book can help you attract such a partner.

But what if you have a partner who is opposed to your starting on your new journey? Who desperately wants the security and comfort that your current job brings in? What if they are quite happy with their lot in life ... and 'why do you need a bigger house, car, more than one holiday per year or to set up a charity? That's for other people – not us, right?' Well, then you need to do one of these four things:

1. Persuade them otherwise – and doing the goal setting exercise can help very much with this
2. Accept your lot in life and continue as you are
3. Do it anyway, but without their support
4. Leave them

Having helped in over 6,000 divorces or separations, I know a little bit about option 4. To help you decide, you just need to answer one question. You have to answer it instinctively, openly and honestly – and you can do that right now.

The question is: *If you won £2,000,000 on the National Lottery this weekend, would you stay with your current partner?* If the answer is 'yes', then that's great.

But what if you answered 'no'? Then you need to find someone who you *would* stay with, irrespective of how much money you have. Because following the advice in this book will set you up with a far better chance at becoming a millionaire. Believe me when I say I am an absolute authority on this, splitting up now will be far cheaper, less stressful and less acrimonious than when you have a business turning over two million per year. Money will not make your relationship stronger. It is more likely to bring in new issues and proliferate existing ones.

If you are having to go for option 3, then you need to decrease the level of risk, increase the likelihood of success and ensure your other pillars are as wide and strong as possible. Because if you have a few attempts at setting up a business and that fails, you will soon have a partner who wants to choose option 4 instead! But if you succeed, then you have the mother of all 'I told you so's – and hopefully a happy partner thrown in for good measure!

My *Relationship* column was the strongest I could have wished for. I was lucky to have a partner who was my cheerleader, my very own 'supporting Sally', my confidante, and who had an absolute and blinding faith in me to succeed, even when I kept failing. It was my own mental health that persuaded me to think I did not deserve such love and commitment. I collapsed my own support column as I genuinely believed my wife deserved better than me. Of course, that was not the case and I hope that poor mental health does not muck up your brain's wiring as much as it did mine. Trust me when I say: there is absolutely no way that I would have a successful business and have achieved all that I have done, without the help and support from my wife. I'd just pulled the wrong bloody wires out!

Work

Some people absolutely love their job and it can keep them going even when all their other support pillars are collapsing. Some careers are better described as vocations; people do them for the love of the job and the satisfaction they get back from that. Consider the cancer nurse who helps with end-of-life arrangements. The vet who gets to work with chimpanzees all day long – or the scientist who helps to develop a cure for HIV. Their work column is strong and they are unlikely to want to change it.

You, however, are going to smash your Work column up into small pieces. But, before you do that, you need to engage with any Supporting Sallies in your existing workplace and think about any potential clients you could use for your new business (without stealing them or going against your employment contract – that's not going to help set you off on the right foot).

You also need to be wary of any work-based Nagging Nigels – and there are likely to be a few who, out of jealousy of you following your dreams, will try to bring you down – as these can take your focus and energy away from achieving what you want to.

There were lots of people in the police who loved their jobs and saw it as part of what makes them themselves. There was even a term for it, 'job pissed'. There were many more who were stuck in a job they no longer loved or wanted to do, but had no other options, no easily transferrable skills and a pension they didn't feel they could give up easily.

You are going to do something completely different with your work column. Rather than it being a column that you are using for support, you are going to destroy it and start a new, amazing column instead. You are going to build this new column on the three others I mention above. You are then going to raise yourself up onto this column, making you and your life even higher. It stands to reason that this column will be thin and weak to start with but, with a strong base below, it can grow tall and wide and provide a base with which to achieve all those goals and dreams and enable you to help others in the process.

It also stands to reason that, with my business three months away from collapse, my Work column was a major contributing factor to my brain crashing down that evening in the hotel in Bracknell.

The next pillar of support can be super strong and can help raise you up and transcend into the next level of pillars you need to build your business on. This pillar is one you would usually pay for and, as you will see in Chapter 12, it is an investment that can make a significant return for you, but only if you get the right people.

Coach or Mentor

People falling under this category include: business coaches, life coaches, wealth coaches, mentors, therapists and counsellors – anyone who can help give you the tools, confidence and encouragement to shoot for the stars. I explain my experience of good and bad coaches in more detail and why my coach and my marketing are now the last two costs I would drop if we had to urgently save money within the business. Having good professional advice from someone who has the experience to give it and is able to do so from a completely honest and neutral point of view is, in my view, vital for your business. It can also be vital to help you be the best you can be for your business. In the Travelodge, I realised I had been completely duped by the business coach I had instructed. I go into more on this in Chapter 11 and discuss how you can avoid the mistakes I made, but to me, it was another column of support that dissolved beneath me and helped cause my brain to implode.

Religion / Higher Power / Spirituality

I refer to this part of this category as 'Religion' and have included it here, even though I am agnostic. It is listed here for a couple of reasons. The first is that there are those who see their religion as being of greater or equal importance as their friends, family and work. They use their religion to support themselves, even without assistance from any other pillars. I am not saying you need to become religious to be successful in business, but it is a support column that those of faith use and find it extremely helpful. Go on any Tony Robbins forum and ask what book they recommend you read. At least half of the respondents will say 'the Bible'.

Also under this category is a column that many people won't currently have but will want to have. It is all part of the journey and your goal setting to develop this column: the support you can get from believing in or supporting something worthwhile. Some people believe in meditation to support them through the day. Others may help a charity, or care for a friend. Yes, the people you help are probably more dependent on you than you are on them at this point, but the comfort you get from helping, supporting or even praying can get you through the tough times. There is nothing like speaking to a rough sleeper who has been kicked out of the emergency hostel because they are addicted to alcohol, to make you realise that deal you didn't win for your business is perhaps not as important as you first thought.

When I was at the Travelodge, I had no such support. I certainly didn't want to start believing in a deity or religion and I had no time or money to help out any charities. But it turns out that, when you do give back, it helps you in a couple of ways. All that positive energy flowing out of you does eventually come back, and can come back in droves. Call it Yin and Yang, or karma or anything else you like, but I assure you the universe has an amazing way of making sure you will be repaid in abundance for the time or money you give.

It can also act as a focus to drive you through when you are struggling. You may donate a few pounds to a donkey charity each month, for example, but having a goal of setting up your *own* donkey sanctuary, in Spain, and helping rescue donkeys that are ill or mistreated – well, that is a whole new level of motivation to drive you through the hard times.

Summary

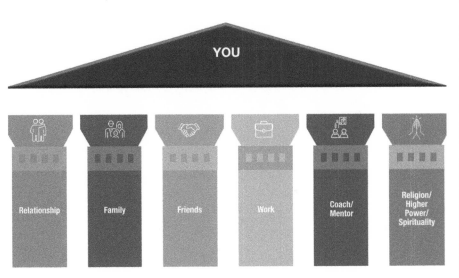

You can see from the above how five out of my six pillars of personal support had either dissolved or weakened considerably, and that the last pillar standing – my Relationship – I had decided would be better placed with another, more worthy, person, due to my depressed brain. It is no wonder that this perfect cocktail of events caused me to hit rock bottom. But, having been there and deciding it is not a particularly great place to hang out, I managed to climb back up again, made sure all six pillars were as strong as they could be and vowed not to let anything like that ever happen again. I genuinely haven't looked back since.

As you embark on your new life, ask yourself the questions: How strong are my pillars of support? What can I do to strengthen them? Who do I need to stop associating with and who do I need to involve more in my life? And, finally, who do I need to ask to coach, mentor or counsel me, to make sure I give myself the best possible chance of success?

'You're braver than you believe and stronger than you seem, and smarter than you think.'

— Winnie the Pooh

2

THE MOMENT THE
WORM TURNED

When I started writing the first draft of this book, I took some days away and rented an Airbnb in Bexhill-on-Sea, East Sussex. I joked that I was visiting 1978, as the town had really not changed that much in forty years, from what I could see. I visited the arcade where my brother, sister and I would spend many an hour trying to win back more 2p coins than we had invested in the shelf-pushing machine; trying to collect liquorice sweets with a grabber that wouldn't grab; getting eaten quickly by ghosts during *Pac-Man* marathons and consistently failing to back the right lane in the blatantly rigged plastic horse derby race.

The outside of the arcade had changed somewhat, and a big sign now said, 'Over 21's only'. On entering, I did a double take. The guy who ran it back in 1984 was still standing behind the glass counter, exactly where I had left him thirty-five years ago. He didn't recognise me, of course, after so much time had passed, so much hair had been lost, a fair chunk of weight had been gained, and – even though I reminded him of my top score in *Track & Field* – he remained relatively unimpressed. I think it was perhaps because I had just reminded him that he had not progressed in thirty-five years and was still doing the same job, in the same place, albeit with different, less fun machines. Perhaps, I thought, my intrusion into his day could be his defining moment. The day when he makes massive and positive changes to his life. But, for now, I just left him looking a bit sadder than before I had popped in. To cheer him up I put two pounds into one of the machines and was devastated to go on to win a fiver. *Could I have made his day any more shit?* I thought, as I hurriedly left the arcade and scampered back to the safety of my apartment.

While this episode turned out not to be the defining moment for him that I hoped my short visit would be, my own defining moment came when I was a police officer and was on the safer neighbourhood team, based in Twickenham.

I was struggling with my life. I was single and living in a one-bedroom flat in Sutton. I had just worked two weekends on the trot due to what we call 'aid' commitments – helping to police events happening in London, such as football matches or demonstrations. I hadn't seen my daughter for three weeks and missed her terribly. I had made a mistake at work with a prisoner's fingerprints, which I had gotten my ear chewed off for, and I was down, lonely and unhappy in my job. I decided to cheer myself up and do something positive. I asked one of the police community support officers if she would like to go on a date with me. It was a stupid thing to do. I didn't really fancy her that much and I wasn't exactly feeling in a great place to go dating, but I thought the worst that could happen was I would have an enjoyable evening out, a nice dinner and, with a bit of luck, some company. I figured she would be chuffed to be asked and that would cheer her up, making me feel a bit better, and maybe the gossipmongers, of which in the police there are many, would let other people know that I was free, single and up for dating. It was a win-win, surely.

It was a lose-lose. When she turned me down flat and asked me if I could help set her up with one of my colleagues, what was left of my precious ego deflated like a sat-on balloon. Fart noises and all. I remember walking back to my car thinking how utterly shit my life was. What could I do to turn it around? I didn't have the answers, so I decided to cheer myself up by driving to Asda and buying myself a bottle of wine and an Extra Special Fish Pie (for one, naturally). I had made my purchase and was walking out past the tobacco kiosk, when I saw a picture on the front of the Evening Standard newspaper, that stopped me in my tracks. *It couldn't be?* I looked closer and saw the headline: 'Candy Brothers Secure Backing for One Hyde Park Development'.

I recognised the name now, as well as the face. It turns out that the chap I used to sit next to in Geography and English had done rather well for himself since leaving our school. Christian and his older brother Nick had taken a £6,000 loan from their grandmother and managed to invest it in a property in Fulham, just at the start of the property boom. Through a combination of imaginative and ground-breaking interior design, they had been able to sell the property at a substantial profit and purchase another. They repeated this successfully until they became *the* property developers and designers of choice for the rich and famous in London. Their brand resonated especially well with the influx of multi-million and billionaire oligarchs from Russia, who were willing to pay well for whatever they desired.

The Candy brothers had become billionaires themselves, had taken the London property market by storm and had been amazingly successful in their lives. I believe it to be a truly wonderful and inspirational story. Meanwhile, the bloke sat next to one of them for two years, while trying to understand Milton and oxbow lakes, was currently holding a £5 bottle of plonk and a fish pie (albeit an Extra Special one).

It was like someone had approached me, tapped me on the shoulder and held a mirror up to my own, pathetic life: 'See what you could have achieved? Do you see what an absolute loser you are now?' It was a *Sliding Doors* moment; had I not gone into Asda, it is unlikely I would have read or even seen that headline and I wouldn't have been able to use that moment of pure shittyness, shining a huge light on the different paths we had taken in our lives, to motivate me to make the change I needed, in order to do something different in my own life.

To top the evening off, I – a qualified chef – burnt the fish pie, making it not-so-extra-special … but I was super busy. My brain was blurring, working in overtime. See, I knew Christian from school. Yes, he was made Head Boy, he was definitely more studious than I was and he was certainly more focused on having a good school life. He was probably more intelligent and had a lot going for him. But he wasn't 'superhuman'. And that is what, up to that point, I had believed it took to become a billionaire. Yes, his story is one that is amazing and I am sure he has worked his nuts off to get to where he is, but I remember the slightly flashy but shy teenager, driving me in his convertible white VW Polo to try and impress the girls at a neighbouring college. I remember a bizarre incident at his house, when his mother accused me of stealing her tiny plastic jug that she used to refill her kettle (I promise I didn't steal it).

But Christian was, well, *normal*. Just like you and me. Ok … fair point … just like *you*. If Christian could become a billionaire, surely I could set my sights slightly lower and become a millionaire? I grabbed a pen and paper. I wrote down on it: *I will achieve £22 million by the time I am 40.* I was thirty-four years old. I signed the piece of paper with a flourish. *That makes it legally binding*, I chuckled to myself as I fell asleep, exhausted, on the sofa.

We now know that day wasn't my lowest point, but it *was* the defining moment I needed to make a change in my life. I didn't know how I was going to become financially secure, or how I was going to make the changes I needed, but I knew from that moment on I was going to make *a* change. Positive, drastic and substantial change. For the next few months, Christian's success was all I could think about. I looked into how he had managed it to see if I could replicate it in some way – I couldn't – and to see if there was something different about him that had made him so successful – there wasn't.

The human brain is an amazing and wonderful thing. Before Roger Bannister broke the four-minute mile, everybody was saying that no one could run a mile in less than four minutes. It just wasn't physically possible for a human to run that distance in such a quick time. Within two months of his breaking the record, which had stood for decades since reliable records began, the record was broken again.

A year later, three runners broke the four-minute barrier again, but this time all within the same race! This example is one regularly used by entrepreneur books to show that what we sometimes perceive as impossible is often just in our minds. But, for me, Christian becoming a hugely successful billionaire showed me that it may just be possible for me to become a successful millionaire. The belief had been firmly set in my brain. I could do this.

'Whether you think you can or you think you can't, you're right.'

— Henry Ford

3

FROM BIRTH TO BONKERS

I was born on a Tuesday in April 1974, in a private hospital in Wimbledon. The hospital was run by nuns, no less. That would prove to be quite relevant later on in my story. Christened Alistair, my nickname growing up was 'Trigg' or sometimes, 'Trigglet'. I grew up in a large, detached house in a village called Ewell, which is in the commuter belt of Surrey, about thirty minutes by train to London. I am sorry, folks, but this is certainly not a rags-to-riches story. My family were painfully middle class. Indeed, I remember asking my mum whether we were lower, middle or upper class and her replying, without hesitation, 'upper middle'. *Wow*, I thought. *A whole new class just for us!*

I had an elder brother, Robert, and elder sister, Caroline. We had a cat and a large garden to play in. We had our own rooms in a lovely house, in a quiet and safe cul-de-sac. I was educated at private schools in Surrey, culminating in my time at Epsom College. I had everything that a child could possibly have wished for and was given every opportunity to prosper in life, except for one, very important missing ingredient.

Love.

Well, to be accurate, love from *both* my parents.

My mother and father did not like each other very much, let alone have much love between them. And my father focused his love and attention on my older brother and sister, leaving me in the cold. My sister and mother compensated for this obvious imbalance, by bestowing even more love and affection on me. I was a mother's boy, spending time in the kitchen, cooking with my mother, while my father would spend time with my brother in the garden. Where I went to the Harrods Food Hall as a special treat with my mum, my brother would go to air shows with my dad. It was a two-pronged approach to parenting. I was raised wonderfully by my mother and disregarded terribly by my father.

While I am not comparing my upbringing with that of many children who have been abused, brought up in households with no love at all and even sexually assaulted, these things happening to you during your formative years does have an impact. No matter what I did to try to garner favour with my dad, I was rejected. I would try to please him and fail consistently. I would do something wrong and would be completely castigated, while my brother would be only mildly admonished. If something went wrong, even if it was nothing to do with me, in my father's eyes it was my fault. I couldn't work out what I had done to be treated so badly by him. Had my father been consistent in his anger and disregard for all of us, it wouldn't have felt so bad. But he was so loving, amiable and obliging to my brother and sister and so antagonistic to me, it singled me out completely.

The sad truth is, my father's love for my two older siblings only served to cast a more obvious light on his lack of warmth and affection towards me. But what could have caused this?

I grew up thinking it *must* be my fault. I must be a terrible child and I was convinced the family would be happier if it weren't for my presence that clearly caused so many issues.

When I was seven years old, I was getting ready to go to school and I did something wrong to upset my dad. He came storming into my bedroom and hit me – hard – on my back. I had red streaks up my back from where I was crouching on the floor. To reiterate: I was seven, and he was a grown man. I'd had enough. I jumped out of my sister's bedroom window onto a metal canopy and managed to climb down a white pole into the garden. I ran down the road and then headed up the A3 towards Kingston. I had no idea why or what I was doing, I just needed to escape.

Walking beside a dual carriageway, at just seven years of age and in full school uniform, I attracted a lot of attention and it was no surprise when I was picked up by a police car just two miles away and taken safely home. For some reason, when I was questioned by the police, then by my mother and finally the school, I didn't mention the reason why I ran away. I have no idea why, but that experience helped to shape me as a police officer twenty years later, when talking to a seven-year-old victim of sexual assault. I knew the words were in there, they just had to be coaxed out.

By the age of ten I had all but given up trying to garner favour with my dad, and like many people do to protect themselves from emotional harm, I built a wall around me. I stopped trying and just tried to become as antipathetic as I could – he could only harm me emotionally if I let him.

But I lived my life with a level of anxiety and trepidation that I now realise was not only extremely unhealthy to a young mind, but was also not the norm. If you have an obvious disability, you can easily compare yourself to others. If you are simply massively anxious, how do you know everyone else in your class is not exactly the same? The bottom line was that I was an unhappy child, in an unhappy household, and while there *were* moments of joy, it is poignant that I cannot remember one that directly involved my father and I.

When I was thirteen years old, I started playing rugby at Epsom College. I loved it. A friend of mine was called Guy. Guy had one eye (love a bit of poetry) caused by ground-breaking treatment of a cancerous tumour behind his right eye. It had been a case of choosing between the eye and the child. Naturally the eye lost. Guy not only went on to become a doctor, he also managed to become a winning jockey at the age of forty-six. A truly incredible feat. But the most incredible thing Guy did, from my perspective, was to introduce me to the local rugby club, called Sutton & Epsom RFC.

The club was my first experience at socialising properly outside of my immediate family. It was a place where I could relax. My anxiety went away when I was there. I saw fathers interacting with their sons on a level that was completely alien to my own experience. *This is how it should be*, I thought. Throughout my teens I spent as much time as I possibly could at the rugby club; I would go training on a Wednesday, see the First XV play on a Saturday, and then Sunday was match day for us juniors. As I grew older, I qualified as a rugby coach and would help out with coaching various teams. To me it was more than a rugby club – it was a sanctuary. My safe place. A place where I felt ... well ... *happy*.

At the rugby club, I met dads who would go on to help me and be mentors I could look up to and respect. One of the dads, Willie Moore, used to smoke and drink and was probably not any parent's idea of a great example. But, in between buying us alcohol at fourteen, letting us smoke at thirteen in his car and laughing at us getting drunk and singing songs in the club bar, he showed me a level of encouragement, belief and understanding that I had never witnessed from the father I had at home. I found friends who I could turn to and share bellyaching laughs with. I learnt about roles in a team, about leadership and inclusivity. My anxiety was such that I was worried it would all end, so I made a point of trying to be the life and soul, the one who would start the rude rugby songs, play the drinking games and try to act the clown. My mother would watch as many of my matches as she could, quietly supporting from the side-lines. My father saw me play rugby just the once – and only because we were heading straight off afterwards on a family trip.

The rugby family became *my* family and that family's highlight was the annual rugby tour. These two, three, even four-day trips were filled with too much drinking, laughing and some of the most outrageous costumes and behaviour you could imagine. The highs of the tour were only matched for me by the hungover, tired lows afterwards. But the memories kept me going for the rest of the year. From missing the ferry home one year because I'd fallen asleep in a ladies' disabled toilet, to encouraging the whole bar to join in a 'trouser round the ankles' fifty-metre sprint up the High Street, if the rugby club was my happy place, then the rugby tour was my nirvana.

This was where I thought my only source of happiness could come from – and then I discovered … girls.

While I had enjoyed a few kisses and endured a few awkward dates and not to mention the horrific experience of losing my virginity, I was relatively inexperienced in such matters.

At thirteen years of age, my brother and I would put on our best clobber and go to the local library hall. The hall often held private parties and events and we would either walk in as though we were a guest or, if the door staff looked on their game, then we would climb through the toilet window. One Friday, we had joined the party via the gents' toilet and I was busy dancing on the dancefloor. Heidi started dancing next to me and doing the sexy bum-touching thing. She wasn't the slimmest of girls, but she said she was fifteen years old and enjoyed dancing. She also said she enjoyed sex and asked would I like to try it out?

I was mature for a thirteen-year-old boy, but had never done anything more than kiss a girl and perhaps a bit of outside-clothes rubbing. 'Of course!,' I replied.

And Heidi led me by the hand to an alleyway by my house. We lay down and started kissing. *'Be quick!'* she whispered 'romantically' in my ear.

Now I had never seen a vagina before, other than on a dodgy blue video that my neighbour played once at a party - and I didn't want to waste this opportunity. The streetlamp nearby cast just enough light that I thought I could get a look.

'Kiss it then.' She sounded annoyed.

What – on a first date? I thought, but not one to argue, I quickly gave her lady parts a few licks and then we awkwardly consummated the brief relationship.

After a few minutes, she said, 'I've got to get back now.'

I hadn't completed my task, but wasn't going to argue, so I zipped up and we both returned to the party.

It was about an hour or so later, when she was dancing with another lad, that I discovered from her friend that I was not her first 'romantic liaison' from the party. My first time ever was only her second of that evening – the first finishing precisely where I had been kissing her. It would be twenty-five years before I would even consider eating a bowl of porridge again …

The horrendous start to my sex life didn't deter my interest in girls, but it did start a pretty horrific run of form.

I was sixteen when I met Annie. We got to know each other through my brother's girlfriend. I thought Annie was beautiful. Her parents were going through a divorce, so I would sit and drink wine with Annie and her mother and we would laugh so hard it hurt. I was in love, ridiculously head over heels in love, and Annie made me happier than I had ever been. Dangerously happy, as it would turn out, because it showed me that this was another area to escape from home to. The rugby club was only open a few times per week. Being in love was constant. I had finally found it. The answer to my anxiety, all my issues, my escape from my unhappy household. It was perfect.

When Annie dumped me after just one month and told me she had a new boyfriend, I was completely distraught. I remember penning her a love note and including lyrics from the musical *Les Misérables* in it (because that's cool, right?), and Annie eventually agreed to go back out with me. Phew, crisis averted – and back to my one constant source of happiness. It is, of course, extremely unfair to put that much pressure on a sixteen-year-old girl. Relationships at that age are not likely to stand the test of time, anyway, let alone when one of you is solely reliant on the other for their happiness.

One difficult occasion was when Annie offered to give me 'a blowie'. At that age, you don't decline such an offer, but I had drunk a few beers at the rugby club and I needed a wee. I took myself off to the toilet and then it occurred to me that, having just had a wee, I should at least give my little fella a good clean, before putting it near someone's mouth. It's only polite.

Not wanting to splash water on me in case it looked as though I had wet myself, I took myself over to the sink, waddling with my trousers and pants around my ankles. I ran the tap and looked around me. The toothbrush mug was the answer I needed! I emptied the mug of the toothbrushes and placed them on the side. I filled the mug with warm, soapy water and carefully placed my penis inside, dangling it into the cup between my legs. This mini bath did the job perfectly and I was confident it would be sparkling clean … *you could use my old chap for a Sherbet Dib Dab*, I chuckled to myself. It was at that point I heard the bathroom door close. Shit. I hadn't locked it!

I am not sure who had walked into the bathroom to see me giving my penis a spa day in their tooth mug, but I know it wasn't Annie as I could hear her in the next room. Needless to say, when I returned the following week, the toothbrush mug had been replaced, along with all the toothbrushes. Awkward.

Over the three years that we dated, on and off, I was a mess. I would drop everything to be with Annie; I ignored friends, even spent less time at the rugby club. I tried everything to keep our relationship going, even though it was simply never destined to survive.

I think the lowest point probably came when I persuaded her that I was perfectly happy just being friends, and went round with a bottle of wine to visit her and her new boyfriend. I just wanted to see her, even if she was with someone else at that time. They soon disappeared upstairs with my bottle of wine, while I slept downstairs on the sofa. Hearing their bed creaks really did not improve my mood!

Looking back now, I can see I was suffering with depression from my teen years. Instead of reaching out and getting help, my way of dealing with it was to try and convince people I was an amazing, happy, confident person. If I could fool them into thinking I was OK, then maybe I *would* be OK. I have a shoe box full of poems that I penned to myself throughout this period in my life. They make depressing reading. But that, along with getting drunk and crying in private, was the only release I had to get the thoughts out of my head.

It was difficult to maintain the pretence and this veneer of happiness. Anyone unfortunate enough to get close to me during this period of time would undoubtedly get hurt by my actions. I just wasn't very well inside.

***

I was fifteen years old when we were sent into Epsom town centre for the afternoon by the school, to survey people as part of our Geography GCSE. I was partnered up with a friend called Billy, but we had an issue. Both my cigarettes and money for a McDonald's were at home in Ewell. We decided we would cycle home, get the ciggies and cash, quickly do a few surveys and have a relaxing Big Mac and fries. Billy and I had both cycled to school, so we rode back to my house in Ewell, about two miles away.

On getting there, I was confident my mum was in, as her car was there and also her pottery teacher's car. Mum was an avid potter at this time and had a studio in the garden. Daniel would come round most days and help her make pots, which they would build, glaze, fire and decorate before selling at local craft fairs and the like. She was a very talented potter. But neither of them were in the pottery studio and the front door was locked. I tried the back door. Locked. I rang the bell. Nothing. I banged the door knocker. Nothing still. In desperation for my cigarettes and cash, I went into the back garden and saw the window of my parents' bedroom was slightly ajar. *I'll scale up*, I thought. Using Billy's shoulders for initial momentum, I managed to pull myself up onto the roof of the conservatory. The same roof I had jumped down from, all those years previously as a seven-year-old, escaping my dad's assault.

Standing on the lead roof, I managed to squeeze my fingers through the gap in the window and flick the latch up to open the window further. I then managed to lift the plume with my little finger, and opened the window fully. Pulling myself through, I jumped directly through the net curtains, landing on the floor at the foot of my parents' double bed.

The scene I was met with was not one I was expecting. Daniel, the potter, was lying naked behind my mum, who was also naked and facing in the same direction. Seeing Daniel slamming into my mum from behind is an image that no child should ever be presented with.

My sharp intake of breath had alerted them to my presence (unlike the bell ringing or door knocking or window opening – they were clearly into their session). My mum screamed and jumped up and I leapt back through the open window, onto the roof and, this time, jumped straight down onto the ground below. I needed to get away from this scene, and quick. I hopped on my bike and cycled as fast I could away.

Poor Billy, who was still standing in the garden, had no idea what I had just witnessed. He also hopped onto his bike and managed to eventually catch up with me. I told him what had happened and made him swear he wouldn't say anything to anyone. I didn't want the news – that I had discovered a ceramics tutor hanging out the back of my mother – to get around the school. Billy suggested I spoke to the school chaplain about the incident.

The chaplain looked completely nonplussed as I recounted the story, listened intently and allowed me to speak freely and openly. Once I had finished recounting the horror show I had just witnessed, his response shocked me. 'Imagine how awful your poor mother must be feeling now?'

Poor mother?! I thought. *I'm the one who saw her being ridden like a bike! What about poor me?*

But this taught me two very valuable skills that I would use later on in my career. I was able to listen to the most horrific accounts of sexual abuse from victims, without showing any disgust or any negative emotion registering on my face. It gave victims the encouragement to keep talking to me. To open up. *What I am saying must be normal to this policeman, as he is nodding at me as I talk.* It worked well.

The other thing it taught me was to always consider how the other person must be feeling. Even though I felt I was the victim in this unfortunate incident, the chaplain's first comment was of concern for how my mum must be feeling. And he was, of course, right. She was absolutely devastated. Understanding that helped me get over the experience, but also helped me when I was dealing with clients at Mediate UK. No matter how poorly they were behaving in mediation, I managed to maintain – in most cases at least – a level of empathy for them that helped the clients get to an agreement.

When I became an adult at eighteen, I was sure my life would improve. I thought becoming an adult, legally being able to do what I had already been doing for six years prior and being able to go out into the world, would cure me of my depression and anxiety. I couldn't wait.

It would turn out that not only was I wrong in that belief, but the following two years would have such a devastating effect on my future that it would take almost two decades for me to recover.

I had dropped down a year at Epsom College to do my A-Levels. The reason for this was that I had taken a year out to go to catering college in London. The idea being: I spent so long in the kitchen already that I would become a great chef one day and run my own restaurant. Spending so much time with my mum cooking was going to pay off large. As an eight-year-old I was gifted cookery books for my birthday, and at thirteen years of age I could dissect a whole chicken into eight separate portions, in under sixty seconds (don't worry, the chicken was dead already).

I was born to be a chef, I thought.

But I didn't get on with catering college as it was far more fun spending my days with Annie, so I bunked off for most of the course. I returned to do the exams and successfully passed my City & Guilds Hospitality and Catering 706/1, from attending about 15% of the year.

My first year back at Epsom College was a difficult one. My attendance record was shocking as I bunked off as much as I could. It just didn't interest me. I disliked the subjects, found the teachers difficult to communicate with and I just preferred spending my time either with Annie or in the local park, listening to '80s songs and show tunes through my headphones. And I'm not even gay!

Towards the end of my first year back at Epsom College to do A-Levels, I was excited to go on a rugby tour with them to South Africa. We were the first British school to tour South

Africa since apartheid had ended. It was a big thing for the school and for us and we had to be on our best behaviour …

But we weren't. The trip was a stressful one as we were losing most of our rugby matches, against schoolchildren who had never had the opportunity to play against another country. They were up for it and, as you may know if you follow rugby, South Africans are fit, incredibly strong and motivated. We didn't really stand a chance. One stay was at a school for partially blind, deaf and disabled children. The rugby ball actually had a bell in it to help them locate it, so we fancied our chances at getting a win against whom we thought would be less-abled opposition.

They absolutely annihilated us. That evening, the teachers all went out for a drink and many of the players did too. I had a splitting headache – a possible concussion from the game – and went to bed early. I got woken up by a loud voice, saying derogatory things about one of our players. I don't know what motivated me, perhaps the headache, the fact I had just woken up, or something else but I got up out of bed and asked the protagonist to "keep the noise down". Turns out you don't tell a drunk, elderly teacher what to do. Certainly not when you are an eighteen-year-old schoolboy. He came up to me and asked, 'What did you say, eh?' I was standing there in my boxer shorts. I can even remember they had red and white stripes on them. He suddenly shoved his hand into my boxers and grabbed my penis. I froze. 'Get to bed,' he said, and walked off. I returned to my bedroom and lay staring up at the ceiling. Did that really just happen? I fell asleep, as we were due to fly to Pretoria the next day.

On arriving at our destination, the decision had already been made. I was to be sent home. Perhaps the teacher had woken up and remembered his sexual assault on a schoolboy. Probably not wanting to be interviewed by the South African police, he instead opted to make an example of me and send me home. I was due to spend a week with a friend after the rugby tour, in what was then known as Swaziland. I still wanted to do this, so I was put on a flight to Johannesburg instead of Heathrow. On the way there, I was escorted by the teacher, who clearly wanted to make sure I got on the bloody plane, and two large burly South African rugby players from our next opposition. It seemed odd that he felt he needed such protection but, as I would discover later from working with numerous victims of serious sexual assault, the protagonists are usually absolute cowards.

Johannesburg in 1992 was not the safest of places for an eighteen-year-old schoolboy who you could not describe as particularly streetwise. This was also pre-mobile phones and communications with my parents back in the UK were not easy. Wandering the street with my bag, I was beginning to attract unwanted attention, so I did what anyone would have done in the circumstances ... I checked myself in to the nearest 5* hotel and got my parents to wire over some money to reception. By this stage, I just wanted to get home – and I arranged to fly home the next day.

On landing at Heathrow airport, I was met by both my parents. My dad was absolutely livid with me. What a waste of money, what poor teachers, what atrocities must I have committed to justify being sent home? The thought that I may have been treated so disgracefully did not factor in his mind at all. This was clearly 100% my fault. They took me for a coffee at a cafe in the airport. I was exhausted from the long flight and just wanted to sleep and to hopefully see Annie. But they insisted and asked me what had happened. Seeing the look of anger and disgust on my dad's face, made even more stark by the contrasting look of love and concern on my mother's face, made me decide I could not tell them what had actually happened. He wouldn't believe me. And it would break my mum's heart. I kept shtum.

This episode was so engrained within me that when I later became a SOIT officer, helping victims of serious sexual assault, all of whom had suffered far worse incidents than my own hairy-handed assault, I made sure my demeanour towards these victims and my composure were that of my mother's that day and not my dad's. My mother knew something was up and spent the next few weeks collating written evidence on what had happened. Many people did not want to get involved. The school did not uphold the complaint that I had been treated unfairly. My mother wanted to raise the complaint to the next level – the school governors – but my father didn't want to. He said it may impact on my education and my ability to get good A-levels. My mother climbed down. I felt my decision not to tell anyone about the sexual assault was justified. If they did not believe I was sent home without reason, which was so clearly the case, then they would never have believed me that I was sexually assaulted by the person who sent me home.

It is not my dad's fault that I didn't tell him about the abuse. But I believe it was his fault that he didn't join my mum in fighting the injustice. He let me down to appease others. Precisely at the time I needed his support, to do what he was good at – writing letters, being pedantic, using his network – he let me down. It is difficult to say whether, had they shown a united front to the issue and not immediately judged that I must be the one to blame, I would have felt confident enough to tell them about the assault. But I am sure the odds of it coming out at the time, rather than thirty years later in a book, would have increased substantially.

It was around this same time that I felt I had to get something off my chest. I had long thought that my dad was not actually my biological father. There were just too many things not quite sitting right, apart from the fact he treated me so dismissively. My grandmother had a photo of him when he was younger and he could have been my older brother's twin. Meanwhile, I looked nothing like him. My mother had already confided in me that their marriage was a sham and she wanted to leave as soon as I had finished my schooling. She had explained that he had rejected any physical contact soon after my older brother was conceived. While I am many things, the outcome of an immaculate conception I am not!

Throughout our lives we had an uncle, who we called 'Uncle Billy' and who was heavily involved in our family life. Billy came on holidays abroad with us. We had a flat in Bexhill-on-Sea and Billy also had one about a hundred yards up the hill. Billy was my dad's boss at the bank they both worked at and my mother was Billy's secretary when she worked there – which is also where she met my dad.

Billy was divorced, had three older children, Alison, Lindsay and Denise and he lived in a flat in Surbiton. He was also, regrettably, an alcoholic, although we children did not know it at the time. We just thought he was extremely funny. Billy was a director at Kleinwort Benson, had a brilliant brain for banking and was well-known and liked in the city. I remember being very impressed that he was included in a copy of *Who's Who* – a data book on people with influence. I adored Billy. He would make me laugh, show an interest in what I was doing and take notice when I spoke. He loved rugby, cricket and cooking. Enjoyed fine foods and was very generous. Oh, and did I tell you, my middle name is William? I had already discovered by then that my mum was not exactly faithful to my dad. Could there have been another affair, before the one I had recently discovered?

I sat down with my mum in the kitchen at our house in Ewell. 'Mum, I've been wanting to discuss something with you for a long time now. I don't think Gerald is my real dad. I think Uncle Billy is my real dad."

She looked at me intently for a few seconds, before a look of sheer relief and gratitude swept over her face. 'Yes, I've been meaning to tell you for years.' My mum then explained twenty-odd years of her relationship with Billy.

She said she was madly and passionately in love with him. Gerald had shown no interest in her physically since my older brother was born, and even laughed at her when she brought it up as an issue in their marriage. She embarked on an affair with Billy, who was also married at the time. She was really keen to assure me that they planned to have me – that I was a 'love child' and very much wanted. That they had planned to divorce their spouses and move in together. Unfortunately, as my mother explained, Billy's drinking got so bad, she felt she couldn't move us three children into that environment. She would turn up to meet Billy and he would be passed out drunk on the bed, lying in a pool of his own urine. Mum explained that she felt stuck and so stayed with Gerald for the sake of us children.

I asked if Gerald knew. 'Well, we never really spoke about it, but he must have done', mum said. 'Uncle Billy paid for your private hospital birth with the nuns in Wimbledon. He paid for your school fees at Epsom College. He came on holidays with us and paid for them, so he could be near you. Gerald wasn't in a physical relationship with me anyway at that time, so there is no way he could have conceived you. He just seemed to accept it, as long as we didn't talk about it or tell anyone else.'

Even though deep down I knew the truth and had confronted my mum with my assertion without prompt, the news still hit me like I had just been slapped in the face with a wet salmon.

I went through a multitude of emotions. I was happy that Uncle Billy was my real dad, my flesh and blood, that I had his DNA, because I absolutely adored him. I was angry. So angry that he had prioritised alcohol over my mum and me. We almost had the chance for us all to have lived as a happy family, not one where I was miserable. I was upset with my mum for not telling me, for not giving it a go with Billy anyway, for telling me how relieved she now felt. I was worried that my brother and sister wouldn't want to be my brother and sister anymore. That they would reject me. I even felt a tinge of empathy for Gerald. My mind was a washing machine of emotions that I'd just switched to a full spin cycle. I decided the best thing I could do was get drunk and go off the rails a little. That'll surely help the situation!

A few weeks later, I was on my way to see Uncle Billy. But Billy wasn't his normal self. On returning from a drunken evening out at the pub, Billy had fallen down the stairs of his apartment block, where he lay for several hours with blood pouring out from his head. Fortunately, he had been discovered by a neighbour and taken to hospital, but he was not a well man.

When I saw Billy, he looked ill and had lost a lot of weight. I told him I knew he was my real father and went in to give him a hug and a kiss. Billy pulled back sharply. He looked uncomfortable. I wanted him to leap in the air and tell me how much he loved me. I wanted him to tell me he was so sorry for all the alcohol misuse and that we could enjoy the rest of our lives together. I wanted him to tell me he was proud of me. I wanted him to love me. But what I got instead was an awkward silence and a physical rejection from my hug. From an emotional point of view, he might as well have just punched me in the nuts.

My whole childhood. Nineteen years of being rejected by Gerald for a reason that I was convinced was my fault. Nineteen years of wondering what I had done wrong. It must have been my fault, as others seemed to love Gerald so much. All that unhappiness could have been averted if Billy had just stayed away from the old red eye for a bit. I was broken.

With the benefit of hindsight, Billy was not well enough to take in everything that was going on, as he was suffering terribly with the consequences from his fall. And it would be wrong for me to point any anger towards him. With the news now out, it did mean I gained a half-brother and two half-sisters. I still keep in touch with two of them.

I believe my mother and Gerald are equally as culpable in the situation. Had they been open and honest with us children and with each other, this could all have been sorted out many years ago. Instead, the need to keep up appearances, maintain our middle-class respectability and keep a stiff upper lip were considered more important than the mental health of what was turning out to be a pretty fucked-up child. It led to legal battles over wills, siblings falling out, angry words being shared and awkwardness at family gatherings. An open and honest approach from the off, could have saved years of confusion and angst.

At the time I perhaps unfairly took Billy's response as another rejection. To misquote Oscar Wilde: 'To be rejected by one father may be regarded as a misfortune; to be rejected by two looks like carelessness.'

'Happiness can be found even in the darkest of times, if one only remembers to turn on the light.'

— Albus Dumbledore

4

THE TERRIBLE TWENTIES

I have an untested theory that your twenties are the most difficult decade of your life. You are trying to find a career, a partner, find yourself even. It was on the back of the Billy bombshell, and heading into my twenties, that my mum divorced my dad. A few months later, she would start a relationship with a piano accordionist, called Trevor Trevani. My dad, meantime, stayed in the former marital home and joined a local line dancing club. My priority at this stage was to get out of the house whenever possible. I managed to get a job as a trainee hotel manager in King's Cross and they put me up in a nearby hostel. The job was awful. I got mugged twice on my way back from a shift, goodness knows what for. I was taken advantage of by the management and was getting paid £60 per week for working at least sixty hours. The street beggar near my digs, with the dodgy-looking dog, was getting a higher hourly rate than I was.

I was told that in five to ten years' time I, too, could become a food and beverage manager for the hotel chain. The current incumbent had taken a shining to me and, on a split shift, took me for a coffee in a gay bar. I only realised it was a gay bar when

I went for a wee in the toilets and saw one man facing north on his knees and another standing facing directly south. I decided I could wait for my wee. But from the conversation it came out that the manager was earning £13,000. I hadn't bothered to look at what a career in a hotel would potentially net me, but I was damn sure that I would need more than £13,000 per annum if I wanted to buy a house and a car one day. I took three days' annual leave and I never returned to the hotel or the dodgy bedsit.

And so would start a cycle of starting jobs, feeling inspired and motivated, impressing as much as I possibly could and then realising I absolutely hated the work, losing all interest in the job and leaving on (usually) uncomfortable terms.

If my employment record was difficult at this time, my personal relationship record was even worse. Anyone who had the misfortune to become my girlfriend during my twenties would have an exclusive insight into my rather fucked-up psyche, the features of which would include, but not be limited to: drinking far too much, feeling down, getting overly excited, ignoring them, doting on them, obsessing over them, being anxious, being overly confident and ultimately being dumped.

From Nicola, who was the sweetest, kindest human being, who I therefore treated terribly, to Angel, who I got engaged to, who desperately tried to help and support me and whose heart I then broke when I realised she was not the one for me. I had neither the emotional maturity, mental capacity nor overall ability to hold down a normal, decent relationship. I was pure toxicity to any poor soul I *did* form a relationship with.

My love life, indeed, perfectly echoed my career, for what that was. Leaving my job as the trainee hotel manager, I managed to get a job working as a chef at a restaurant called

Gavvers in London. It was the site of the Roux Brothers' original restaurant, Le Gavroche, which they subsequently moved, retaining Gavvers. The job involved split shifts in London, so I would leave home at 8 am and get back at 10 pm. It was tough work. I would spend my time de-stoning a 5kg box of cherries, or peeling the middle section from partly frozen prawns. Service was chaotic and busy. A wooden peg would drop down the hatch from the restaurant above. '*Ça marche, trois couverts*, one chicken, one duck and one salmon.' I was on salmon. It was rushed and chaotic, and I didn't get the gratification I craved from preparing the dish. It was then that it struck me. The reason I loved cooking and preparing food for others was the acknowledgement – the thanks, praise and recognition – that I received. It wasn't the enjoyment of making the actual food that drove me to being a chef. It was the attention I received from serving food to friends and family that was my driver. It was also one of the few times that Gerald acknowledged I was good at something.

My time at Gavvers was made tougher by the fact I was bullied by the chefs whenever the head chef was absent. Their favourite pastime was to ask me to get something from the bottom of the fridge and then take the long-stemmed candle lighter, used for lighting the gas hobs, and burn my ass with it as I was bent over. They found it hilarious. Me, having worked a twelve-hour shift in a hot, sweaty kitchen, less so. The final time they did it, I twisted round quickly and suddenly and punched the offender as hard as I could (which to be fair wasn't very hard). I walked out and never returned. With that punch went my desire to ever work in a kitchen again. It is of great credit to the Roux Brothers that, even though I was only there a short period of time, they conducted a full investigation into the situation. I still have a signed cookbook from Michel and Albert Roux as an apology. I was put off from cooking as a living, but they helped develop further my love of good food and, if nothing else, the importance of pairing a great rouille on a bouillabaisse soup.

It was on a rugby tour that I was introduced to Blodders. Blodders managed NatWest Bank Sports Club and was after some help in the kitchen and with running the place. Having vowed never to work in a kitchen again, I somehow immediately found myself back in a kitchen. This time it was less 'traditional French gastro for the city elite' and more 'microwaveable meals for retired bankers'. In the end, this was never going to be a long-term career and I left, but not before I had helped cater for the chavviest wedding offering in South London.

Where most venues would charge in excess of £30 per head for the wedding breakfast and a drink, NatWest Bank Sports Club were offering a three-course wedding banquet with a drink for just £12.50 per head. Bargain. Most brides opted for Menu A, the roast turkey (frozen rolled joint and sliced thinner than a sheet of toilet paper). But on this occasion the bride had gone for Menu C: Lamb noisettes at £15.50 per head. Proper food, requiring proper cooking!

We ordered the noisettes in and served them grilled, just pink, on a raspberry jus, with turned courgettes, carrots and mini roasted potatoes. It looked the nuts. Unfortunately, the guests were not used to such cuisine and the feedback was mixed. From 'my one's not cooked properly,' to 'I thought lamb chops had bones in 'em?' to 'Can I have some ketchup with my nuggets?' Perhaps it was little shock when a couple of the guests took it upon themselves to go and get a takeaway from

McDonald's – not just for them, but for the whole wedding party.

The small room they had booked for their reception now stank of greasy chips and ketchup; the floor was covered with empty chicken nugget boxes, while the bride was crying her eyes out in the corner. Matters then took a turn for the worse when it was time to cut the cake. The bride's best friend had made the two-tier wedding cake for them and carefully covered the fruit sponge with a layer of marzipan and then royal icing. But she may as well have set it with creosote. This thing was harder than Chuck Norris. We kept calling for larger and larger kitchen knives, until we ended up apportioning the cake into splodges using the meat cleaver. By this time the bride was too drunk to care and was shouting at her new mother-in-law about how her family and friends were a 'bunch of McScumbags'. I'm not sure that marriage would have lasted the duration.

The job did lead to one of the funnier moments in my short-lived catering career. We had a new chef join us for a busy shift and after a few hours you could see him shifting uncomfortably around the kitchen. Rather than walk, he would shuffle his feet and was in obvious pain.

'Are you OK?' I asked.

His face showed he was not OK and, after some prompting, he explained that his arse was burning raw from a heat rash. It is not uncommon to get a sweaty arse in a hot kitchen and, with the constant movement, this can lead to an uncomfortable and itchy rash. In the absence of any Sudocrem or talc to help the condition, I spoke to the Head Chef, who suggested this poor chap use the baking powder from the store.

'You're having me on?' But no, Chef insisted that it was a well-known trick in the industry. Baking powder acts like a talc and will absorb the sweat and help the rash. It made sense. My sweaty arse friend grabbed a bowl of powder and took himself off to the changing rooms. He was gone for a good five minutes … where could he be? Ten minutes passed, still no sign of him. Eventually the Head Chef and I went to look for him in the changing rooms. We didn't expect to see what we found.

Sat on a heavy porcelain sink with his trousers and pants round his ankles was this poor lad, clearly in agony. We could see the tap was running behind him and he was splashing water on his arse using his hand in a swiping motion behind his back. He looked up. 'You bastards!' he cried. 'I knew this was a wind up.'

I moved closer and could see his arse looked like a giant, hairy tomato. It was burning red.

It turns out he had mistakenly taken a bowl of cream of tartar – an acidic powder made from the by-product of wine production – and covered his already sore rash in it. He may just as well have sat in a puddle of bleach. I like to think that my instant reaction is to help in such situations and to show empathy and compassion to the victim. But, to my eternal shame, I fell to the ground laughing. I don't think he ever returned to work at the kitchen.

Having given up on cooking as a career, I decided I wanted to work in an office environment. It must be less stressful than a hot, sweaty kitchen and the idea of getting paid while seated somewhat appealed to me. I applied for over fifty jobs and was rejected for all of them. Eventually I got an interview with Reed's who had a contract for providing customer service agents to Lombard Finance in Redhill.

I was to spend six years at Lombard, who dealt with financing cars, before being merged into First National. I started off on customer service, progressed to the help desk, which dealt with more specialised cases, and then got promoted to a trainee business analyst. By the time I was in the project management department I had completely given up on the job.

I hated it. I did not understand it and I had also had the misfortune of falling head over heels in love with a girl there. Julia was stunning. Everyone could see it and everywhere she went she attracted attention. I befriended Julia and we became close. While I made it clear I wanted a proper relationship with her, Julia explained her ex-boyfriend had badly hurt her and she was not ready for a new relationship. I didn't know at the time that that is a massive red flag and a sign to stay the fuck away. I put everything I could into my relationship with Julia. I took her out for lunch, treated her to dinners, she would stay over at mine and we would drink wine and listen to music together. We even went to London to the theatre and stayed overnight in a plush hotel. But we were never intimate. She kept explaining how she wasn't ready to commit to a relationship. I racked up thousands of pounds in debt trying to win her favour. In my mind, Julia would eventually see that she was meant to be with me and all my effort would have paid off. Julia made me happy, amazingly happy, and if she would just commit to me, I was sure she was the key to unlock all my dreams and cast aside all the depression and anxiety. It didn't happen. I remember one of the managers saying rather bluntly to me, 'You should have just bought a Rolex, it would have been a cheaper accessory on your arm'. Ouch! Painful, but true.

Eventually and perhaps unsurprisingly, matters came to a head and we fell out. I had nothing to show for the non-relationship other than a broken heart and a credit card bill in excess of £5,000. A few weeks after we fell out, I was speaking to a colleague in another department and she asked if I was OK with the news about Julia. The news? It turns out that Julia was dating someone else in the project management department. The same department I worked in. Strangely enough, she felt ready to commit to a relationship with him at that time. I could hardly believe it. I genuinely believed her when she said our issues were just a matter of poor timing. I left work a few minutes early and got in my car. I remember it was, perhaps fittingly, absolutely sheeting it down with rain. I drove round the one-way system and parked my car up opposite the designated smoking area by Sainsbury's.

Sure enough, at five minutes past five, Julia came out. She walked straight up to her new boyfriend and flung her arms around him and gave him a kiss. I had been desperately hoping for almost two years to have a moment like that with her. My heart was crushed and I drove back to my home in Sutton a broken man. Letting myself into the house, I curled up in a ball and cried for hours. I saw it as another rejection from someone I loved and that evening was the first time I contemplated committing suicide. I got as far as writing the note, which I carried around with me for a few months. But the whole experience affected me terribly and ultimately influenced my decision to get married a few years later.

By my final year or so at First National, I was made a team leader for a new department. The experience was horrific as my line manager was a complete and utter asshole. Everyone knew he was an asshole and I was warned before I applied for the job, but I needed a new challenge and more cash to pay off my 'Julia debts'. The asshole manager never really gave me a chance. Putting more and more demands on me, he wanted me to organise a new unit, while taking the staff on a day trip for a team-bonding exercise. It is difficult to bond with someone you want to head-butt every time you see them, but I tried. The experience was a terrible one and led to my having a massive panic attack, upon which I was admitted to hospital. It served one purpose, and one purpose only. I remembered every negative interaction with 'the asshole' and did the exact opposite when I started managing a team again, some twenty years later.

By the end of my tenure at First National, I was on a project to reform the business. I had no idea what I was doing. I was placed on a small team to come up with the reporting requirements for the management, including for the asshole. It had something to do with data warehousing. Well beyond my comprehension. My day would involve coming in at 9 am and reading emails and the company intranet until 11 am. At 11 am I booked myself out for an imaginary meeting until 12 pm. Between 12 pm to 2 pm I could get away with not being at my desk, as it was lunch time, and I would book in another imaginary meeting at 2 pm to 3 pm, returning to my desk for the last two hours of the day. By doing this, I had freed up four hours between 11 am and 3 pm during which I could drive the two mile journey back home and play games on my computer. I was completely demotivated and demoralised in my work. And it didn't help that my mental health was so poor that, when I explained all my symptoms to my GP, he immediately signed me off work for a whole three months.

I remember being called in to work during this period of sick leave, as my manager and HR wanted to check on how I was doing. I suspect they believed I was faking it. On turning up to my interview, they took five minutes before deciding they shouldn't really be talking to me at all and sent me packing. Yes, I came across as that downbeat and scary!

It was during this period that I decided I needed a proper career, one where I could make a real difference and enjoy the job. At that time the police were undergoing a huge recruitment drive. I spoke to my friend Matt, who was in the police at that time. He let me come out with him on a shift and I was immediately in love with the job. This is what I wanted to do with my life. Chase bad people, help good people. A proper Robin Hood, just without the dodgy green tights.

My decision to join the police corresponded with a national campaign to recruit more officers, so I applied and amazingly got through the interview process and, more importantly, the background checks.

A potential problem I had was that, when I was nineteen years old, I had been arrested and received a police caution for 'criminal damage'. Except I hadn't actually committed any criminal damage. I and some friends had returned to my house in a drunken state from the rugby club and decided to try and make a giant pyramid from all the wheelie bins in the road. Not an easy task, and not a particularly quiet one, and so one of the local neighbours called the police. The trouble we had was that, just as the police turned up, one of my friends took it upon himself to swing from the local hairdresser's canopy and it broke.

We all ended up getting arrested for criminal damage. These days I would have known exactly what to have said to ensure I didn't receive any conviction, but back then at nineteen, I had no idea and I was completely blindsided by the arresting office being called 'PC Shufflebottom'. Instead of concentrating on getting out of the police station and out of trouble as soon as possible, we immediately set up a game where we said the arresting police officer's name as much as possible and tried to do so without laughing. Sure enough, we all received a caution (which you can only get if you admit to the crime, which I hadn't) and I was fortunate that this had now come off the police records after two years and before I applied to join the boys in blue.

I had to miss a good friend of mine's stag do to Barcelona that summer, as I had my fitness bleep test and medical. Feeling nervous about passing these tests, I couldn't sleep the night before. I was still awake at 4 am and I couldn't get to sleep no matter what I tried. So I decided to do what any man in his twenties might do in that situation. I had a wank.

That moment of self-reflection worked and I managed about three hours' sleep before I was up and getting the train to the recruitment testing centre in London. Immediately on arrival, I was asked to provide a urine sample in a tube. It was to be used for testing for drugs, along with serious medical conditions that may impact my ability to be a police officer over a twenty-five-year career. Pissing into the cup and decanting it into the tube was difficult enough, but my face turned a bright shade of crimson when I put the lid on and there, floating in the tube, was a whole load of my semen, like at a Lido on a summer's day, happily swimming about in my urine and making it appear a little cloudy.

To this day, I have never been so embarrassed as I was handing over this creamy-coloured urine sample to the medical staff and I fully expected the report to come back that I had a protein overload issue, or to just be labelled as a potential pervert to watch out for.

By this time in my life, I was twenty-seven years old and I was living with a family in Belmont, Surrey. I had met them through the rugby club. The dad of the family was affectionately known as Tony 'Fucking' Gordon, or TFG for short. TFG and his family took me in as a lodger at this difficult time in my life and looked after me. I was friends with TFG's sons, especially David who worked as a manager at the local nightclub (handy). TFG understood me. I had worked with him on coaching the Under 19s at the rugby club. We bonded over that, but I felt our relationship was so much more. Tony could see that I was a complete mess and struggling with doing life. But he didn't try to cure me or tell me to snap out of it. He just helped me and talked to me and was there for me. He was a father figure like no other. What Tony didn't know was, I was constantly on the verge of going into a deep, dark depression. Tony, his wife Ricki and their friends and family kept me going through one of the darkest periods in my life.

It would be only a few years later that I would be on police duty when I received a call to say that Tony had died of bowel cancer. I was so proud that Ricki asked me to conduct his eulogy at the funeral, which was attended by over 300 people. I did OK and didn't fuck it up. It was the least I could have done for the man. For Tony's family, his premature death must have been like a shot through the heart. I was delighted to hear many years later that Ricki married another friend's dad who had also lost his wife to cancer. I could not imagine what Tony's wife and family felt, but to me it was simply a case of another father figure who I adored coming into my life and then leaving me. Even typing this, I have tears in my eyes over the memory of a man who just 'got me' in a way no other father figure had done before.

In May 2001, I found myself heading to Ireland and to Waterford for a friend's wedding. The event was set over three days and it was going to be huge! Everyone from the rugby club was attending and the couple getting married were amongst the nicest, funniest and friendliest people I had ever met. I felt Jacko and Niamh had done things 'the right way' and I admired them hugely for that. Meeting at university, they had been together for many years before getting engaged. Jacko had worked his way up through various banks in the city and was doing well in his career. He would go on to do extremely well and move to Singapore and then Hong Kong with HSBC. A fantastic couple, for whom, through my own selfish mental health issues, I almost completely ruined their wedding without them even knowing.

About a month or so prior to their wedding, I started dating a girl – we'll call her Natalie – and I really liked her. I think she realised pretty quickly that I was not all the ticket within myself, but we started going out and Jacko agreed that she could come to Ireland as my plus-one. A kind gesture, typical of the man, while trying to organise a huge wedding weekend in another country.

We drove to Ireland but things with Natalie were not going well. There was an atmosphere which I couldn't work out. Despite this, we were heading for a great weekend away in one of my favourite countries in the world – what could possibly go wrong?

The wedding was to be on the Saturday morning. The Friday was spent fishing and in the evening we all went out to the local nightclub. It was there that I saw Natalie happily snogging one of my close friends. Another rejection! And from both my friend and then girlfriend. In a rage, I stormed up to them and went to punch my friend, not the best of ideas as he was about twice the size of me and as we have already discovered, I don't have the best of punches.

I think the bouncers threw me out and I was left standing on the street. At this point one of Natalie's friends came up to me and started attacking me. Slapping me in the face. I looked at the bouncer as if to say, 'what can I do?' I had no idea why I was being attacked and I was certainly not going to get involved in a fight with a woman. The bouncer told me to just walk away and so I did. As I walked along the dimly lit roads, I let the tears flood down my face while my brain started with its negative tricks. 'They are all going to laugh at you tomorrow.' 'Of course Natalie wanted someone else, you are a terrible person, after all.' 'Your friends will all side with Natalie anyway as no one likes you.' 'It's time to finally put an end to all these rejections.' 'People will have a far better time if you are not around.'

I walked the couple of miles back to our villa, where the fish I had caught was now starting to stink the whole place out. In readiness for my and my friends' hangovers we had bought a few packets of paracetamol between us. True to form, I consumed at least three packets of pills and anything else I could find lying around the villa. The alcohol I had already consumed gave me the confidence and encouragement to go for it. I downed more booze that was lying around. In my drunken state I then managed to get a taxi to the airport, where I intended to try and buy a ticket home. My reasoning was it could make repatriating my body easier and have less of a negative effect on the wedding party. Yes, that was how fucked-up my brain was at the time.

Arriving at the airport, I looked around me at a fairly deserted foyer before I collapsed on the floor where I was standing. I passed out. The combination of alcohol and pills had taken their toll and I was taken to hospital by ambulance. In hospital they ran some tests and put me on a drip. I can't remember much else of what happened but was aware I had a tube down my throat, so I presumed I had my stomach pumped as I had a terribly sore throat when I came round. In the morning, I woke up and immediately regretted my actions. Shit, I had to get back, changed and get myself to the wedding. I called the nurse and explained I needed to discharge myself. She was not happy to let me go until I had spoken to a psychologist. At 9.30 am, I saw the on-duty psychologist who I managed to convince I wasn't going to go straight out and try to harm myself again.

As I exited the hospital, I saw a friend, Adrien, from the rugby club. 'Trigg – what are *you* doing here?' Fuck. He had come in with a sore wrist and caught me completely by surprise.

'Umm, I drank too much last night and passed out. Ended up here.'

'Shit, Trigg,' he said. 'Take it easy, you could have killed yourself!' I didn't mention that had been my intention.

I got a taxi back to the villa and quickly showered, shaved and got dressed. I made it to the church just in time to see Jacko and Niamh get married. I had gotten away with it.

My depression continued when we arrived back in the UK. Natalie was determined to carry on her campaign against me, and she slept with another friend and then finally my then best friend. Having confided in my best friend what had happened at the wedding – I was living with him at that time – I felt completely betrayed. It ruined the circle of friends I had at the rugby club and destroyed my friendship with him, who had been like a Siamese twin to me through my late teens and twenties. And while we would later both attend each other's weddings, our friendship never really recovered from that. I just added him to my list of people I felt had rejected me.

So it was from a very bad place that I started my training at Hendon in November 2001. It was just two months after the 9/11 attacks and the security level in London was at its highest possible setting. We were told that, even though we were a few weeks in, we may be called up to help out if there was an attack on London. I just wanted to use the whole police experience as a chance to reset and have a new start. By this time, my relationship with Gerald was beginning to improve. He had remarried and he even agreed to come to my passing-out parade with my mother and sister. It was a proud moment. Finally, at twenty-seven, I had actually achieved something. I was a warranted police officer, proclaiming my duty to the Queen and I passed out second-best overall from our class. With this accomplishment, maybe I could build a relationship with Gerald. Maybe, finally, he would be proud of me.

At the end of my time at Hendon, I was introduced to Karena at a local, cheesy nightclub, called the Chicago Rock Cafe. Karena was only nineteen, some eight years younger than me, but she was pretty and kind to me and we arranged to go on a date. I took her to an Italian restaurant in Sutton, where she ordered a mozzarella, tomato and basil salad, but without the mozzarella. I thought that a little strange but I persevered. She had a bandage on her right arm that she said she got from kickboxing. I would later realise that the ordering of just a sliced tomato was part of her eating disorder and the bandage was covering up her scars where she had self-harmed. But Karena doted on me and I desperately needed that attention.

Unfortunately we were both toxic personalities to each other. We had terrible arguments and would split up on regular occasions but Karena always came back to me and wanted to make me happy. I knew by this stage she also had mental health issues – she was far more open than I was with her struggles. *That's it!* I thought. This was my answer, at last. What if I could help Karena to overcome her eating disorders, her own mental health issues and her anxiety and depression? Surely that in turn would make me happy and surely Karena wouldn't hurt me like Annie, Julia and Natalie had? I didn't let on to Karena about the full extent of my own mental health issues, I just wanted to help her get better. Then I would have done something worthwhile and in the process, I would overcome my own issues. It was, I thought, an amazing idea.

It was, with hindsight, an absolutely horrific idea. Our relationship was harmful at best, self-destroying at worse. Regardless of splitting up on several occasions and then getting back together again, we got engaged and were married with a wedding in Sutton and a reception in Weybridge, Surrey.

The wedding went fine, other than that it was tipping down with rain. As we arrived at the hotel and checked into our rooms, Gerald approached me and handed me an envelope. I didn't have time to open it, but I thanked him. My mum had already given me a cheque for a thousand pounds earlier that week so when I did my speech, I thanked her for this but didn't thank my dad for his – as we still had not had a chance to open it. This compounded with the invitation of my half-brother and sister (Billy's children) to the occasion and an absence of thanks in my speech for him raising me – see earlier in the book for the reason – was taken as a massive personal insult. I had embarrassed him in front of everybody and he, quite wrongly, believed I had done so on purpose. A few months later, he wrote a letter to me telling me this and explaining that he didn't want anything to do with me ever again. He asked my sister to return to me any photos and personal memories he still held of me.

I didn't see him again until my brother's wedding a few years later. By this time, Karena and I had our daughter, Amelia. I politely said hello to Gerald, while holding Amelia, who was about four months old. As I started to introduce him to Amelia, he turned his back and snubbed my baby girl. My brother-in-law, who was standing beside us, was so shocked at the vulgarity of the snub, he let out a gasp of 'Wow!' It would be the last time I saw Gerald and the last time I would ever allow him to reject me. I could take the rejection of myself, but not that of my baby daughter.

Gerald died in December 2021, just after his 91st birthday. I felt desperately sad for my brother and sister on the death of their dad. But I personally felt nothing inside and that shocked me. I had clearly put to bed any feelings I once had for him. I felt I could have been a good person in his life. I felt I could have benefited him and him me. Instead, when he died, I had not seen or spoken to him for almost sixteen years and, if nothing else, that is just a very sad situation.

Gerald did manage to provide one last 'fuck off', which sums up the man he was. In producing his will, rather than just stipulating whom he would like to leave his estate to, he made sure to specifically request that none of his money reached me. I wouldn't have wanted or expected a penny. I learnt so much from him on how *not* to be a father, how *not* to treat others and where my priorities in life *should* lie. You simply cannot put a price on that.

My marriage to Karena was only one year in and already it was in deep trouble. We were making each other miserable. We decided, in a final attempt to rekindle things, to move to Essex, to the same estate where my sister lived, and we bought ourselves a new-build, small, detached house. Surely that would make us happy? No, two months after moving in and on 1st January 2006, I found out that Karena had joined various sugar-daddy dating sites and it was the excuse I needed to do what was obviously required. I wanted to separate.

As I have since discovered is relatively common, Karena's family and friends gathered together and tried to ruin me. One of them called the police station I was currently attached to, to say I was drink-driving into work every morning. Another called the police to report me for having child porn on my computer and Karena herself would later report my stepson for sexual assault on Amelia and accuse me of domestic violence to child services. It goes without saying that none of these allegations were true. All were timed to cause maximum embarrassment and disruption to me or my new family.

Karena returned to Sutton and I remained living in Essex until the house could be sold. I managed to combine working shifts in the police in Romford, with seeing Amelia in Sutton. I would collect her from Sutton on my days off and drive back to Maldon in Essex. While the drive was tiresome, the time I spent with Amelia made it all worthwhile. I absolutely loved being a dad to her.

Amelia almost died several times, during what was a horrific birth. However negative my feelings towards Karena would become, I will never forget the admiration I had for her bravery and determination over a gruelling twenty-four-hour period to deliver Amelia safely into the world. Amelia had the umbilical cord wrapped around her neck and was positioned at an angle. Every contraction was squeezing life out of her and we only realised how close she came to dying after she had been safely delivered in the theatre. Her heart stopped on more than one occasion. To my awe, Karena had saved our daughter's life before it had even begun. I am eternally grateful to Karena for that. And I would allow that fact to cover up for every subsequent negative incident that occurred between us.

As soon as she was born, Amelia was handed to me; Karena was far too exhausted and had just been prepped for an emergency caesarean. Amelia took one look at me and screwed her face up as if to say, 'What the fuck was all that about?!' But as soon as I saw her, a wave of love came over me that I had never experienced before. I had a daughter and my heart completely melted. It was a major shock, a reset. I was now a dad and I had to put my own 'dad issues' behind me. Someone else needed me now and needed me to be a better person.

Having Amelia in my life was one of the major contributions to my coming out of my depressive twenty-something years. I felt I needed to man up. To be a better, stronger person for her. I didn't do anything as positive as get professional help or counselling, of course, but I had someone relying on me to be OK. Amelia forced me to become better within myself and I am extremely grateful to her for that.

As her mother and I separated when she was just shy of her first birthday, I could console myself that Amelia knew no different to the situation and I was grateful when Karena got into a new relationship with a police officer, whom I hoped would help her and provide support for Amelia.

I loved the time I had with Amelia as a child. My new flat in Sutton was full of pink toys, a huge doll's house, pictures of Amelia. She kept me going and I remember once when it snowed heavily; we could not return Amelia to her mum's and I could not go to work, so I had an unexpected extra day with Amelia. A snow day! We played in the snow for hours and enjoyed such a memorable and fun time together. It is those unexpected and unplanned situations which you remember the most. Her mum might have saved Amelia at birth. But Amelia most definitely saved me.

Just eleven years after her birth, Amelia would tell me that she never wanted anything to do with me again. That she hates me. She has never been willing or able to explain why.

Her mother had a failed suicide attempt when Amelia was ten and it is possible she blames me for that. Amelia struggles with her own mental health – hardly surprising given her combined parentage – but at the time of writing, she has declined to see me or hold any meaningful contact with me, her half-brother or stepbrothers for six years. I have missed every single day of her teenage years.

It may be that her mother's family have brainwashed her, it maybe she struggled with having a mum and a step-mum and feeling torn, or it may be that her mother turned Amelia against me over the years and I am a victim of child alienation. Whatever the reason, it is simply not usual for a child to suddenly reject a parent in such an extreme way, without justification. I had doted on Amelia. The situation wholly and utterly broke me.

Being rejected by both your fathers, is one thing. Being excluded from their life by your own, first-born child is a whole new level of rejection. It is fair to say that I feel part of my heart has been ripped from my body. The only thing that keeps me going is one day, maybe, Amelia will need me in her life again and I will need to be there, at my best, for her. Unlike my own experience of fatherhood, this father's love will never die or falter. I use that every day to try to become a better person for when she is ready for her dad to be back in her life again.

As we'll discuss later, trying to find the positive in every negative has become a crucial part of my journey to being happy. I use this experience and all the unfavourable feelings from my own background to try to help other people. I work with both mums and dads to parent their children better when they go through divorce or separation. I use the void Amelia has left to focus on becoming successful enough in my life, that I am able to fund a charity to help teenagers with their mental health.

The pain of this experience has driven me to grow Mediate UK to the company it is today. Finding the positives in the negative motivates me to keep achieving more so I can give more back. For now, it is all I can do for my daughter.

'Every adversity, every failure, every heartbreak, carries with it the seed of an equal or greater benefit.'

– Napoleon Hill

5

CAN YOU SMELL BACON?

I absolutely loved being a police officer. To start with, anyway. It is without a doubt one of the most difficult, sometimes dangerous, but highly rewarding and worthwhile jobs there is. The vast majority of police officers join because they want to help others, not, as many people would tell me, because they were 'bullied at school'.

A police officer will run towards a danger when every natural instinct is to run away from it. In any given shift, you could be having a roll around on the floor with a disgustingly smelly shoplifter, taking an initial allegation from a victim of rape or telling a family that their child has been killed in a car accident. I did all those things several times, but fortunately never in the same shift.

When I joined the police, I was based in Richmond and Twickenham, not the most horrific of London boroughs, but enough to keep you busy. I was put on a response team and I would look forward to every shift.

I spent two years on probation before I got a chance to complete my response driving course, which – let's face it – is one of the main joys of becoming a police officer. The course taught me one important lesson, not just for better driving, but also for life… to raise your vision. I'll come on to the implications of this later in the book in Chapter 20.

One of the common things we would deal with in the police is dead bodies. I must warn anyone here that they may find the following difficult reading, especially if you have lost someone in tragic circumstances. Every sudden death in the UK has to be investigated, at least initially, to ensure there has been no foul play. If I never see another dead body again, it will be too soon. Our first body we dealt with was when we were probationers shortly after we were let loose on the public. A builder was working in the basement of a property with dangerous chemicals and the fumes overcame him. He passed out. He then spent some time breathing in the highly toxic chemicals until he unfortunately died. As chemicals were involved, the fire brigade, or 'water fairies' as we called them, had to be involved. Us probationers were called and took it in turns to see our first ever dead body. When my turn arrived, I was led down to the basement. I saw the body lying under a blanket on the floor. They asked me if I was ready and they slowly lifted back the blanket to reveal the pale face of a man, in his late forties, early fifties maybe. He seemed perfectly at peace and I thought it was not such a bad experience to have this as my first sudden death.

At this point the corpse's eyes opened and he jumped up at me, shouting 'Waaaah!'

I'd like to be able to say that I reacted coolly and calmly to this. But instead I screamed a high-pitched scream that would deafen a dog. What I didn't know was that the body had already been carried away to the morgue and my 'corpse' was one of the firemen, who had agreed to play a prank on me as a probationer. Absolute buggers.

I was not so lucky on my next few dead bodies. These included an old man who had died peacefully in his sleep while watching the TV. Unfortunately the heater was on beside him and that made his body rot quickly and go particularly smelly. He had been there for several days when we forced entry to check on him, following calls from a concerned neighbour. The stench was so bad, I rushed to the window to open it and let some fresh air in. I put my hands together to part the blackout curtains, only they weren't blackout curtains I was trying to pull apart. They were black flies, resulting from maggots on the deceased. I didn't fancy my food much that shift.

Another occasion, we were called to search a property, where a high-risk missing person had been reported. The house had already been searched once, when he was first reported missing, but to no avail. Several days later and he was still missing, he required medication to control his mental health and his family and friends were getting more and more worried.

We did a cursory search of the house and then started searching in hidden places such as the wardrobes, the garden shed and, finally, the loft. The loft was accessed from the landing, via one of those hatches that you push with a stick to open the latch. Standing on my tiptoes, I racked my baton out and, reaching up, I could just about touch the hatch with the metal bulb of the baton. With a small click, I managed to push the hatch up and released it to allow it to open. The next thing I knew a pair of trousers were dropping towards me and my natural reaction was to catch them. It turns out that the poor man had chosen to hang himself from his loft beams. As the body decomposes, all the fluids drop down the body as they are no longer being pumped around. When you hang yourself, gravity really kicks in and the body is often elongated as a result. You will often see dead bodies of people where they have hung themselves with their knees drooping just about at floor level. They weren't like that at the moment of death. This poor chap had been in a warm loft and he had elongated – a lot.

Catching a dead body by the legs as it falls out of a loft hatch is not something that happens every day to you. Even to this day, when I open a loft hatch, any loft hatch, I instinctively stand to the right or left, just in case someone has decided to hang themselves up there.

Perhaps the worst 'sudden death' I dealt with was when we were called to a flat in Mortlake. The downstairs neighbour was concerned for the safety of a neighbour upstairs, as water was coming through her ceiling. We arrived at the flat and knocked loudly on the door. Nothing. We tried to enter the door but the lock was too strong for my size nines. We called for the door enforcer, a heavy metal object used to smash quick entry if you are doing a drug raid, for example. Once inside, I rushed to the bathroom. There in the bath was a naked lady, about the same age as me. I instinctively dropped down and picked her up out of the water. She was rock solid. I can still recall the feel of her cold clammy skin on my hands. Rigor mortis had begun to set in. This poor lady was a diabetic and having not been feeling well had decided to run a bath. Once in the bath, she had a diabetic fit and passed out. As she was in the bath – she slid down into the water and she drowned. I looked around the apartment. There were cards lining the shelves saying, 'Congratulations on your Engagement'.

It was at that point that her fiancé came running into the flat. At this stage, he is a possible suspect for murder, until what has happened is unquestionably clarified. In theory, he shouldn't be contaminating a potential crime scene. But try to tell that to someone who has just seen their dead fiancé in your arms. I have never seen the pain of grief etched so clearly and deeply onto someone's face, as on his that morning. He blamed himself as he knew his fiancé was feeling unwell but went to work anyway, with her full encouragement. Her family also blamed him. One month later another team were called to the same apartment. The fiancé had killed himself. They were both twenty-eight years old. It goes without saying that such things affect you; you would be a complete robot if they didn't. I couldn't even have a bath for many months after that incident and chose to shower instead.

Dead bodies were not the only smelly things I had to deal with during my time. On a shift in Wimbledon, we were called to a fight outside a pub – a common occurrence and one that is never fun to deal with. Most people are usually drunk and expect you to know the detailed history leading up to any incident upon arrival. They can also turn rather nasty and dangerous quite quickly.

On arrival at this scene, I could see there was someone with blood stains on their face and shirt and I could see someone clock us arriving and make a run for it in the opposite direction. Not having fully established what was occurring, but not wanting the perpetrator to get away, I ran after him. Amazingly, I managed to catch up with him, tackled him to the ground and cuffed him behind his back. It was textbook, just as we had been trained many times before. I told him he was under arrest on suspicion of assault and Section 5 of the Public Order, as he was also swearing and shouting in the street. I searched him, as is usual after making an arrest, to make sure he had nothing on him that could harm him or us and, as I patted his trouser pockets with the back of my hand, a smell wafted up to my nose that could only be human excrement.

'Oh fuck, I've shat myself,' he complained to me.

At this point, the incident in the pub had been resolved and the person responsible for punching our blood-covered victim had been arrested inside.

'Why did you run from the police?' I asked this soiled chap.

'I was running home as I was going to be late. My missus will kill me!' It turned out that the suspect I had pursued and tackled vigorously to the ground was not running from the police at all. He was just running home so as not to face the wrath of his wife. About 500 yards into his journey home, he had been rugby-tackled to the ground by someone, handcuffed and the shock of this, combined with the alcohol he had imbibed, had made him shit himself.

Oops. I quickly de-arrested the poor man.

'You can't de-arrest me now,' he pleased. 'Please nick me again so I have an excuse to give the wife.' I explained that I couldn't do that and that he would have to walk home now.

'The least you could do is give me a lift?' He had a good argument there, but the thought of him stinking the response vehicle out, combined with another call we needed to attend to, meant I had to apologise and leave him to walk home, covered in his own faeces, to his presumably very angry other half. I wrote my notes up very carefully that evening, but fortunately the complaint never arrived. I do wonder if they are still married.

After my time on the response team, I transferred to the Sapphire unit that dealt with serious sexual offences. My role was to act as a single point of contact with any victim of a serious sexual assault and take them through the stages of the investigation. The key role being to support the victim, obtain forensic evidence and help compile their statement, hopefully leading to an arrest and conviction. I would then support them through any subsequent court trial and keep them updated throughout. We would be on call in shifts, and would often get called out at two or three o'clock in the morning to attend a scene.

I was trained in a technique called ABE (Achieving Best Evidence) interviewing, where we would video the account of what happened, and I went on to become advanced ABE trained, meaning I could take statements from children under five and mentally handicapped victims of serious sexual assault. It was a challenging job to say the least, but when done well, it was amazingly rewarding. I much preferred dealing with a victim of crime, rather than a dead body. The victim was still alive, still had everything to live for, and their courage could help us put away a rapist or paedophile.

I discovered I had a natural empathy for the victims I was called to, and I was good at engaging with them. We would need to take an initial statement from the victim, check for any forensic opportunities and then support the victim, who had just been sexually assaulted. For most cases, we would need to persuade the victim to drive with us to a secure forensic examination at a place called The Haven, in Camberwell, where they would suffer further, albeit necessary, indignity.

On arriving at the Haven, specially trained nurses would take intimate swabs from the vagina, mouth and, if relevant, anus. Any bruising, scars or damage were recorded on a rather crude sketch of a vagina or anus. They would have their blood taken, be given emergency HIV prevention pills, the morning-after pill and a referral to a sexual health clinic. If necessary, they would have their tampon bagged up. I would then be responsible for transporting the victim back home and then painstakingly checking-in all the exhibits into the secured fridge or freezer. Recording each exhibit in detail, as continuance of evidence was key to any successful conviction. On one occasion, having asked the victim to sit on a white sheet in the back of the car, while I transported her to The Haven, the only drop of DNA we managed to find from the perpetrator was from that sheet that I had subsequently sealed in an evidence bag, after she sat on it. I got a commendation for that piece of foresight.

A tampon could provide great evidence as a sponge for any DNA and we would be required to wrap the string around the top of a small white pot and leave the tampon hanging in the middle of the pot, before screwing the lid on. The actions I took could help convict a serial rapist and I knew that if I mucked up and a case was subsequently dropped or lost at court, due to lack of evidence, that I could be responsible for more women being raped. It was a huge responsibility for a young man still in his twenties, but my careful tampon evidence helped secure a conviction for one of my victims.

Another important part of the role was to take the statement from the victim. These would be several thousand words long, covering pages and pages of paper, or even hours of taped video interview. You can't foresee what defence a suspect will come up with, so you need to cover everything in minute detail. The smallest fact could prove to be the difference between a conviction or not. You may know how few cases of rape are successfully prosecuted, every detail in both the statement and in evidence collection could be the item to make or break a case. I took my job seriously and worked hard to do as much as I could to strengthen the chances of a conviction for every victim I worked with. It also showed me how incredibly strong and brave they were during the subsequent investigation and court case.

I am proud of the fact that I never had a victim of sexual assault say they did not want me, a man, to deal with their case. I gave myself two minutes to make an impression on them and for them to know they could trust me. It worked. I helped prosecute a serial rapist, a paedophile and several cases where the rapist was well known by the victim, including members of their own family.

Performing such a challenging role takes a toll and after a couple of years, I could feel myself becoming desensitised to the repeated horror of these accounts. This was the point at which I felt I needed to do something different. Plus, I was married at this time to Karena who was pregnant with Amelia and she hated me doing the role. I left and moved to a Wimbledon response team, where my love of the job started to go rapidly downhill.

It was difficult going from dealing with serious sexual offences back onto a new team. I would transfer from Wimbledon to Romford, during my ill-fated move to Essex and then back to Richmond, where I would end up on the safer neighbourhood team and had the privilege of being able to see all the key rugby matches and concerts at Twickenham stadium. But even with those perks, I had by now lost my love of the job.

I knew I had to get out when I was approached one day by a group of cocky youths in Twickenham town centre.

'Ere – can anyone spell bacon?' one said out loud, as they walked past where I was standing. I quickly stuck my arm out and held my middle finger under his nose. 'No, can you smell your mum?' His friends all burst out laughing, but he didn't appreciate my gesture. It was unprofessional, confrontational, and I was a thirty-something-year-old man making a mum joke to a teenager. I knew then I could not continue in the role.

At the time I blamed the changing rules and culture in the police, but in reality, the problem was 100% me. I was frustrated because I wasn't doing what I loved. Yes, even one of the best jobs in the world is not going to work out for you, unless you love doing it.

How do you quit a secure-for-life job, with an amazing pension scheme, which will support you and your family should anything bad happen to you? Well, I will explain all that in Part Two. But first I need to share with you a love story …

'Keep smiling, because life is a beautiful thing and there's so much to smile about.'

— Marilyn Monroe

6

A LOVE STORY

Chhristmas 2008 was a particularly shit Christmas. I was up early to drive to Karena's flat to see Amelia open her stocking and presents. We had been separated for almost three years by this point. At lunch time, Amelia went down for her nap while Karena and I shared the most awkward of Christmas dinners. The atmosphere was so frosty, I left shortly after lunch and returned home to my flat. I spent the rest of the day alone, drinking wine and watching reruns on TV. At least I had Boxing Day to look forward to. I was going to meet up with my family and enjoy swapping presents and good food. However, the next day the snow came and our Boxing Day was cancelled.

I spent the time between Boxing Day and New Year mostly in my underpants playing computer games and generally just smelling bad. I forced myself to go out on New Year's Eve – the first time in nine years that I was not working in the police on this day. I should explain that my anxiety goes through the roof when I walk into a room full of people. When I was a student at Roehampton University (for a whole month) we had a freshers' trip to the Ministry of Sound in London. I lasted about five minutes before I had to leave. Even now, I find it difficult walking into a room full of people at a party, bar or club.

I thought, *well, New Year's Eve – I am bound to get a least a snog at midnight from someone.* At 12.10 am I found myself walking back to my flat, snogless and feeling down on myself. *My New Year's resolution,* I told myself, *is to take positive action and join a dating site.* On the first of January, probably along with a load of other people, I signed up to match.com.

The first thing that happened when I signed up was that I matched immediately with three members of the ladies' team from my local rugby club. *I could have saved myself sixty quid and gone to the club instead,* I thought. Match.com were doing an offer whereby if you signed up for six months, you got six months free. I went for it. A whole year of dating was ahead of me and I was convinced I would find someone willing to snog me, at least.

Neither of the first two dates I went on were a particular success. One used photos from eight years prior and, while I tried to make it work, we just didn't connect. The second date was with someone I knew from my teenage years at the rugby club. She reminded me of many stories of my antics as a teenager, none of which I could really remember and she looked particularly unimpressed when the waiter bought over the card machine and I pretended it was a mobile phone, holding it up to my ear. 'Hello? Hello … there's no one here, mate.' I don't think the waiter was particularly impressed either.

January rolled into February and I received a message from someone called Amber, from Woking. Amber hadn't come up on my radar before then, as I hadn't set my search area that wide but, as I would later discover, Amber had set her search radius to 'national' as she could only afford to subscribe for one month and needed to find her man! We exchanged messages for a little while, and then phone numbers, and finally arranged to meet up just after Valentine's Day 2009. I was in a positive mindset as I drove to Woking for our first date.

I had been to a friend's funeral from the rugby club that week. Kelly was a beautiful person, both inside and out and we had been romantically involved for a little while. She was sent home from her job as a teacher with a splitting headache and, just hours later, was rushed to hospital, where she died from a brain haemorrhage. While her funeral was not exactly an event to put anyone in a good mood, her sudden death showed the importance of treating each day as though it could be your last. I was determined that week to do just that. I arrived in Woking and knocked on the door. My heart immediately sank. I must have been catfished. The lady who answered the door was at least ten years older than what I was expecting, and her hair was styled like a badly assembled bird's nest. What was I going to do? Fortunately, matters were quickly resolved as we both established that I was at the incorrect address.

I drove round the corner, parked up in the visitors' bay and knocked on the door. Amber answered the door and, well, my heart sank again. Standing in front of me, smiling from ear to ear, was the most beautiful woman I had ever laid eyes on. This was going to be a complete disaster. Amber was far too good looking for me. I would be faced with another Annie, or even worse, a Julia!

Amber invited me in and explained her babysitter was running late. 'That's fine', I said – we could order a Chinese if need be. Amber seemed relieved at this suggestion and it helped calm our nerves. The babysitter *did* arrive, and we went to a local restaurant. We chatted away all evening; it was relaxed and comfortable and I was determined just to enjoy my evening with this woman, who I would never have the confidence to approach in normal circumstances. Amber's conversation was kind and entertaining, and I thought it especially charitable of her to invite me in for a coffee when I dropped her back to her house. I mean, she clearly isn't interested in me, but how nice she's done that. We chatted over the coffee and then I got up to leave. I believed wholeheartedly I would never see her again and wanted the evening to end on a high before I said or did something to fuck it all up.

I had enjoyed a fantastic evening with a gorgeous lady and I just wanted to count my blessings. I went to give Amber a peck goodbye on the cheek and we ended up having a full-on kiss. I pulled her closer to me and, yes, she was definitely kissing me back. I didn't think she had drunk that much? The thought flashed through my mind that I may be on some sort of American style wind-up prank show, but no, I was actually kissing the most beautiful woman I had ever seen in my life and she was definitely kissing me back! I was euphoric.

On my way home, Amber sent me a text message to say how much she had enjoyed the evening. I was on such a high, I had to pull over onto the hard shoulder of the A3 to compose myself. I replied, saying I had enjoyed a wonderful evening and I hoped to see her again soon. All my barriers and anxiety came crashing down. If I was going to be hurt by someone, fuck it, let that someone be Amber, because I would sacrifice anything to see that beautiful smile again. That weekend, I arranged to send Amber flowers which wouldn't arrive until the Monday. On the Saturday I got a message. *Hey, my sister and I are eating Haribo, and having a competition to see how many we can fit into our mouths. Wanna come over and join in?* Absolutely. I joined in and I lost.

Amber and I moved in together eight months later, got engaged twelve months later and married two years later at a wonderful venue in The Cotswolds that we had hired for the weekend. We were surrounded by all our friends and family, our children and our dog, Stormie, was our ring-bearer. For me, it was the perfect weekend, marrying the perfect woman.

Amber had two sons, from previous relationships: Bailey who was then six years old and Dempsey who was just about to turn two. Bailey and Dempsey's dads didn't want to have anything to do with them. I now had three children counting on me to be a dad to them and I was determined to step up.

Bailey's biological dad's hobbies included weightlifting, taking steroids and snorting cocaine. Dempsey's dad only showed an interest in his son when he wanted to stop paying his child maintenance. At the time of writing, both dads still owe child maintenance payments. From my viewpoint, there was never any question that I wanted to be a father to these two young boys. We nicknamed Dempsey's father 'Wanky McShitdad' after he took Amber to court for child arrangements for Dempsey, only to tell the judge he didn't want to see Dempsey again as he found the whole thing 'too difficult'. It was never about Dempsey, it was about his seeing Amber again – and when he saw that we turned up to the contact centre together, he withdrew his court submission.

Even when I had no income and, under child maintenance rules, I was not due to pay anything, I was determined to pay child maintenance each month for Amelia. It was the first bill paid. There were only two months when I was unable to make a voluntary payment, which I describe shortly. Bailey's dad, on the other hand, had to have a court order and bailiffs sent to collect payment. His mother even contacted us to try to persuade us to drop the child maintenance claim. In desperation, he requested a DNA test, which cost him a further £400 and came back as a 99.99997% that he was Bailey's biological father.

Bailey will admit he wasn't the easiest child to raise. Amber recalls the time when, at just five years old, Bailey was sat waiting on the stairs for his dad to collect him, bag packed and excited for a night away. Tony never turned up to collect him. I knew only too well that rejection like that can have a severely negative impact on a child's mental wellbeing. For my part, I promised myself I would always do three things for the children:

- Love and support them
- Be 100% honest with them
- Help them be the best versions of themselves

I didn't always get it right. But I am so incredibly proud of all my children and seeing them overcome adversity. Tony seemed less impressed with my raising his child for him. Some twelve years into my parenting relationship with Bailey and having proudly just helped him buy his first car, I received a message from Tony:

Like my money do you ya fat little cunt. Why don't you try getting a real job to support your family instead of living off me. How you getting on with ya £71,000 debt you fucking loser. Why don't you come and meet me tough guy!..

The irony was, I got the message while flying back from Miami, where I had just been upgraded to First Class. I'm not sure where he got £71,000 debt from, but I presume he mistook it for 'creditors paid' on the company accounts.

We decided to show Bailey the message as part of our promise to always be open and honest with him. I think he had some choice words for his dad in return, but I didn't rise to it. Tony clearly has many anger issues he needs to address and I genuinely hope he does address them and at some point in the future can be a positive in his, now adult, son's life.

Dempsey's dad, meanwhile, is too busy ducking his responsibilities and hiding from the Child Maintenance Service to be the father he needs to be. I don't think it has affected Dempsey in the same way as it did Bailey, as Dempsey never had any relationship with his dad to start with. Dempsey has asked questions and, again, we have always answered honestly and openly. The saddest part is that Dempsey is one of the most talented, kind, gifted and genuine boys I know. I get to be his dad every day - how lucky is that?

With hindsight and given both their emotional flaws, it was perhaps a blessing that both dads disregarded their parenting roles.

Meanwhile, Amber had made me the happiest I have ever felt in my life. Twelve years later, she is still the most beautiful person inside and out. Our relationship is built completely on laughter, love and respect. I genuinely am the luckiest guy to have Amber in my life, but she had presented me with a problem at that time. I now had three children to support and a wife who I needed to feel I was worthy of being with. I needed to leave the police and set up my own business. It was the only way I could fulfil the life I wanted for us all.

'Love your family, work super hard, live your passion.'

— Gary Vaynerchuk

PART TWO

BUILDING A BUSINESS

7

THE FALSE START

As I walked down the long corridor at Twickenham Police Station, I felt a lightness and feeling of relief wash over me. It felt like someone had floated down from the sky and had lifted all the stress off my shoulders and was gently massaging my deltoids. My footsteps felt far less heavy on the floor tiles than they had on my walk in the opposite direction ten minutes earlier. Yes. I had just handed in my notice to quit the police. A job I had held for almost ten years and which I had moved from loving with a passion to hating. I felt so good, so much less stressed all of a sudden and so relieved, I must surely have made the best decision of my life. Right?

By the time I had reached the end of the corridor, the reality of what I had done, struck me. *Fuck! What HAVE I just done?* It suddenly dawned on me that my next pay cheque would be my last. As I walked out into the yard, I saw a couple of response vehicles flying out for an emergency call. I looked on and wondered if I had just made the biggest mistake of my life.

I phoned Amber. 'I've done it, I've handed in my resignation … bit scared now.'

Amber replied, 'You have done the right thing, you hated the job and are destined for so much more.'

'I hope so. Thank you for all your support, I won't let you down and I will get you that lovely house for us all to live in very soon. I love you.'

My plan to run my own business had taken a few twists and turns in the lead up to my resignation. Initially, I was going to run a sandwich shop from Woking, called The Great British Sandwich Company. I had staked out various locations and done footfall counts on them. I had settled on this empty space near to Woking station. I had plans to theme each sandwich with a famous British person ... fancy a Beckham on wholemeal, anyone? And I was going to build up the business and then franchise it. I wanted to be like Pret a Manger, but based on good, locally sourced British ingredients.

Then I worked out the upfront costs. I would need at least £20,000 to get the shop up to scratch, get the marketing and staff trained. I had £250 in my account. The idea was over before it had started.

However, a new opportunity had come my way. I was aware of a local café on our patch at Twickenham, called The Scrummery. It was a rather dated café which the owner only opened on match and event days at Twickenham Stadium. Her name was, by an unfortunate coincidence, Karena – and I had met with her and agreed that I would take over the running of the café during the time it was normally closed and that she would continue to run the Twickenham match and event days.

My plan was to use my contacts with the safer neighbourhood team to distribute thousands of flyers to the students at the nearby college when they attended their freshers' week. The safer neighbourhood police usually have a stall at such events to give advice on personal safety and the dangers of drugs etc.; my plan was to include some Scrummery vouchers in with the *Just Say No To Drugs* leaflets. Simple!

As we approached the day I was due to take over, Karena approached me with a different offer. She was (quite rightly, as it turned out) concerned that I wouldn't make enough to live on from opening outside of event times, and offered that I could also take over the events.

She wanted £28,000 p.a. for the rent and use of the equipment. I managed to haggle her down to £23,000, on the basis that we were new and there were fewer home matches that year at Twickenham. I honestly thought I was Lord Sugar with my negotiating skills as I drove home and I called my mum to tell her the good news.

My mum had always wanted me to have a career in catering, following on from my youth spent in the kitchen, and she was delighted for me. I was on a bit of a high driving home, when I saw the lorry in front of me smash into a Mini and then just carry on driving. I could see in my rear view mirror that the Mini driver was female; she had got out of her car and seemed to be fine. She was quickly surrounded by help. *I'm not having that*, I thought, and pulled up alongside the lorry. I could see the driver very clearly and I was flashing him and trying to get his attention. He was having none of it. I called the police and explained what had happened, while I followed the lorry driver into a depot. When he got out of the lorry, he tried to run off into one of the buildings. He was about twice as large as me, but I managed to hold him by one arm while I was on the phone to the police. Suddenly I was surrounded by five or six Eastern European men, all having a go at me for holding his arm. It was all getting a bit scary. I marched the lorry driver to a nearby wall to limit his escape options and turned my back for a moment while I spoke to the police operator to give her the lorry's registration number. During that brief intermission, another driver had joined us and, as I turned around again, I could see they were midway through trying to swap shirts.

I lost it. 'You, get the fuck away from him now, or I will have you nicked for obstructing a police officer … you …', pointing at the lorry driver, '… if you so much as move, I promise you I will fuck you up.' Now, he was about six foot two and could give Popeye a good arm wrestle. I'm five foot ten in Cuban heels and not exactly known for my physique. Also, as it turned out, he was completely bladdered. By now, I had just upset a group of very angry, very aggressive and very drunk Poles. As they all looked at me and started walking towards me, I considered my options. Obviously, I was going to bravely run away, but where would be best? I saw my car about twenty yards away and reckoned I could peg it to that and then lock myself in until help arrived. No hero award for me this year. Fortunately, at that moment Surrey police arrived on scene and nicked the driver, who it turns out was three times over the legal limit, while driving a 32 tonne artic. The matter ended up at court and the driver was banned from driving and deported back to Poland. I believe the lady driver managed to get some money back to cover the damage and, other than the shock, was completely unhurt from the crash. It would be my last ever involvement in a crime as a police officer.

Aside from detaining drunk lorry drivers, I was extremely busy in the weeks leading up to the grand re-opening of The Scrummery. I had no money, or experience of marketing, so my great marketing plan was to have some balloons put out at the front of the café to grab any passer-by's attention!

I had hired an assistant manager who, despite a long CV of working within the catering industry, was happy to take on the job at just £7 per hour. I also hired a cook, who assured me she was an amazing chef and that all of her friends frequently invited themselves over for dinner at hers as her food was so delicious. She was currently retraining at catering college. Finally, we hired two younger assistants on a part-time basis. One wanted to be an actress and had read that everyone in Hollywood started off working in a café before being discovered, and the other girl needed a job while she was getting ready to go to university.

We were a motley bunch and in the week leading up to opening, I spent twelve to fourteen hours per day buying the food and drinks we needed to sell, collecting kitchen items, getting floats and tills ready, printing menus and pricing up items. It was knackering but exhilarating. I was about to run my own rugby-themed café!

The day before opening, I was busy in the kitchen preparing a homemade lemon cheesecake, a gingerbread cake, rocky road and various other homemade treats. I returned home at gone midnight, exhausted, nervous and just a little excited.

I got to The Scrummery early the next morning and remember rolling down the awning to show the café was open. The awning was stiff and difficult to manoeuvre. I smiled to myself as I started singing: 'Awning has broken, like the first awning …' We pumped up balloons and tied them outside on the railings. We folded napkins into pretty shapes. As I turned the newly bought door sign to show 'Open', a sense of pride came over me. Now we just had to wait for our first customer.

We waited. We waited a long time. When our first unfortunate customers *did* walk through the door, we were so pleased to see someone that we pounced on them like they were alien lifeforms visiting us from a nearby galaxy.

The first day, we made a little over £20. Still, start small and think big and all that. We had, at least, started. The first week, I had hoped to turn over £1,000. My plan was to use this to help fund the beers, food and other stock needed for the first rugby international in just over one month's time. Instead, we took a little over £100. Not even enough to cover the staff wages. I had to do something and do it quickly.

I rustled up an offer for three 'gourmet nights'. Three courses for £10 (yes, really); I printed the menus and we placed them in letterboxes on all the neighbouring streets. My plan was to entice them in with an unbelievably good offer and upsell them to the steak (£2 supplement) and good wine (£10 profit per bottle). I invited friends from the rugby club too – they didn't disappoint and duly booked their tables.

The gourmet nights were a success in terms of turnover (not so much in terms of profit) and, despite finding out that the trainee chef couldn't cook for toffee, with the help of a loan from a good friend I had enough money to buy beer, sausages and food for the first international and to just about pay the staff wages.

The night before the first international, I could hardly sleep. Karena had agreed to join us to show us the ropes, with some of her family helping out. The catering could be split into four key parts:

1. The cooked breakfast. People booked tables and had a full English breakfast. We served teas, coffees and orange juice with this.

2. At 11am we flipped to lunch. This was usually some form of hotpot or easy to serve main course. We sold tepid cans of lager with this, and, my brilliant new idea, bottles of wine.

3. As the crowds started milling past, we fired up two BBQ's at the front and sold, 9" hot dogs, with bacon, friend onions and chilli sauce.

4. Finally, to catch all the post-match hungry visitors, we offered bowls of chilli and garlic bread. The idea being to make the chilli really hot to appeal to the macho rugby player and also to get them to buy more cans of tepid lager at £3 per pop (plastic cup included).

Even with the experienced Karena helping out, it was absolute mayhem. The electrics kept blowing; the food was average at best; our manual table booking system had been lost; my assistant manager had neglected to tell me the reason he couldn't get any other job in the industry was that he was a functioning alcoholic and, in between him having a big fall out with Karena, was hiding glasses of wine around the café – leading to him being hopelessly pissed by the end of the shift.

I finished mopping up the last puddles of spilt warm lager just after midnight. I got home and counted up the takings. We had taken just under £4,000 in the day. I could pay the staff, pay back my friend who I had borrowed money from and just about buy food, beer and wine for the following week. I flaked out, having never been so tired in my whole life.

It became clear quite early on that The Scrummery was not going to make a profit during the week. After having to sack the assistant manager, I hired a new chef/manager and both he and his girlfriend worked out much better.

The next two months were busy with the October internationals and trying to promote The Scrummery for some trade during the week. Geography played a part in the issues we faced. The café was on a red route and had no free parking anywhere nearby. In a largely middle class residential area, most people were at work or drinking coffee in trendy cafés in Richmond or Twickenham. As the year drew to an end, I made the decision to only open over the weekend. We were just making too much of a loss during the week, and throwing all the unsold food away was heart-breaking.

It was during this period of free time during the week that I came up with the idea of food delivery at the weekend. If people couldn't easily come to us to eat, let's take our breakfasts to them! 'Breakfasts in Bed' delivery was invented, and I had a thousand leaflets printed.

We spent ages circulating these to homes within two miles of The Scrummery and even had a surreal conversation with Pete Townshend of The Who – he was based in Richmond and he wished us luck in our new venture! Following my chat with Pete, I was taking a break from delivering leaflets when I had an inspirational idea. One of the issues with our breakfast delivery was that we had to cook the food and get it to the customer while still hot and appealing (fried eggs do not make a good travelling companion) and we never knew how much food to buy.

If we bought too much, we had to bin it as we only offered the service at the weekend; too little and we would have nothing to sell and annoy most of our – very hungover – breakfast clients. I knew that several of the cafés in Twickenham already offered a really good selection of breakfast items. What if I could persuade them to let us use our delivery and advertising to sell their breakfast products? We could have people order through a website and get cyclists and moped drivers in branded uniforms. We could expand it to all restaurants and offer a service throughout the day. We could call it 'Deliverme', as a play on the word 'delivery'. It was genius.

> *But no. It would mean asking restaurant and café owners to work with us. They may say no, and we know that rejection is something I wouldn't take well. They may laugh at my idea and think it stupid. Plus I don't have the marketing knowledge, the money or knowledge on how to build a website. It's probably best I stick with delivering cold scrambled eggs to people too hungover to complain!*

And that, ladies and gentlemen, is my story of how, following a chat with a rock legend, I almost invented Deliveroo. Exactly two years later, Deliveroo *was* started – about three miles away from Twickenham. In 2021, the business floated and was valued at £7.6 billion.

Now, back to The Scrummery. We had a couple of home rugby matches to keep things ticking over, but we were running out of cash – and quickly. The café was taking about £50-£100 per day on the weekends when there was not a rugby event at the stadium. That meant 95% of our income had to be derived from Twickenham event days. Those days, therefore, had to run as smoothly as possible, as there were only a few such opportunities during the year. I soon learnt that we had to maximise the income from the BBQ at the front, as this had the highest profit margin. I would wake at 5 am on event days and get back past 1 am, when we would count the takings while stinking of fried onion and bacon grease. I'd gone from a job where people would continually accuse me of smelling of bacon to one where I genuinely did and horrifically, stink of bacon!

The stress of it all was making me ill. I knew that we would run out of money at the end of April and we would have four months with no major events being held at the stadium. We were fucked. I got through the April and May fixtures as best I could and then had to let everyone know that we couldn't continue with The Scrummery. I was in a mountain of debt and knew I could not pay the rent to Karena at the end of the month.

My first business venture had failed after just nine months. I felt I had failed – and failed miserably. I went into hiding and shut myself off from the world, with debtors chasing me for money.

But what I *did* have was a nine month crash course in business and marketing. I since discovered that the rent, which I thought I had done so well to negotiate, was double what the other shops on the parade were paying each year. I never stood a chance and some simple research would have shown me that. So I learnt the importance of doing research before committing to a contract. I also learnt how to get people interested with an outstanding offer and then upsell them more once you have their attention. I learnt how to hire and fire people. I learnt how to manage people to get the best out of them, even though I was only hiring them for a few hours every few weeks. I learnt about profit over turnover, cash flow, stock management; and I learnt an awful lot about myself and my ability to work incredibly long hours in difficult and stressful conditions. I hadn't made any money. But I hadn't lost a load either. And I had just completed the learning equivalent of a business MBA in nine months. I had to take that as a positive.

At The Scrummery, my best clients had been my former police colleagues. Some would say it was one of the safest places to be in London at the time! Once I was no longer running the café, I had an interim offer from my old chief inspector, who asked me if I would run the canteen at Twickenham police station. In the absence of any other offer, and coming up with the great idea that I might be able to run 'breakfast in bed' from the police canteen in future, I accepted. For the next six weeks, I would get up early and cook bacon sandwiches, make coffees and serve sandwiches to my former colleagues. I would package up sandwiches for the late shift and leave an honesty box for them to buy the sandwiches from a cooler in the late afternoon and early evening. Thieving bastards that they were, I don't think the honesty box ever tallied with the merchandise!

But after six weeks, the chief inspector called me over to apologise. He had been told by Scotland Yard that they could not hire me to run the canteen, as another outside catering company had an exclusive contract with the Met. I had to leave that day.

I packed up my stuff and called Amber. 'Hun, I can't continue at the nick anymore. I've got no job or business.'

I could hear the panic in her voice. 'Oh my God, what are we going to do?'

'Don't worry … I'll think of something.'

'I know you will – I love you.'

'I love you too.' I ended the call and, turning around, I could see two response vehicles leaving for an emergency call. I realised I was standing in exactly the same place I had been in when I had just handed my notice in and was wondering if I had done the right thing, only nine months earlier. Except this time I cried behind my sunglasses, as I felt that I had let my wife down and let down the three children I had promised her I would support. I believed I had fucked everything up in less than one year.

But then something strange happened. My tears dried up suddenly and I could feel my shoulders arching back and my spine straightening. The sun was beating down on my face as I came to an amazing realisation. For the first time in my life, I was completely free. I had no commitment to be somewhere at a certain time. No need to run round like a nutter buying frozen sausages and packs of bacon. No need to be on duty at 10 pm for a night shift. No one telling me to do things with a data warehouse (to this day, I still don't know what one is).

Instead, I was completely unburdened by anything or anyone. And I could do whatever I wanted to do. I *was* going to start a new business. I *was* going to make it a success and I *was* going to make my wife and children proud of me. I *was* going to put aside all the shit I had dealt with in my life and be someone that would make others proud of me and, perhaps more importantly, would make me proud of myself. I had been a (fairly average) chef, a phone handler, a business analyst, a police officer and, briefly, a café owner. I had pretty much hated and failed at each and every job. But I was going to set up a great new business. I was going to make it work. I had greater expectations for my life and was going to see them come to fruition. I just had no idea what I was going to do, yet. But in that moment, I knew I was destined for better things and that this unexpected firing was a sign, pushing me forwards.

I strolled with purpose to my car, loaded it up with a crate of leftover egg mayonnaise sandwiches and headed back home. I gave myself six weeks to come up with an amazing business idea that would transform my and my family's lives.

It took me just four weeks – and a random news bulletin on the radio – for me to decide what it would be.

'If you really want to do something, you'll find a way. If you don't, you'll find an excuse.'

— Jim Rohn

8

MEDIATION, MEDIATION, MEDIATION

I n the weeks following the demise of The Scrummery and my short-lived police canteen venture, I decided to continue reading as much as I could about business. I read books on start-ups, self-help books, books on investing, finances, everything I could get my hands on. I read about goal setting and the importance of this in a business but also the importance of personal goals. I'll share my insights on goal setting in further detail later but I made myself three goals at this stage.

1. I would buy my wife and children a beautiful house we would all live in.
2. I would write a book of my life experiences and call it 'Greater Expectations'.
3. I would have a net worth of £22 million.

I wrote them down to commit them to paper and I made a conscious effort to open my mind up to every opportunity I could find. I had read that business is just about solving a problem and doing it better than others. I looked at everything. If I was eating, I would look at every part of the meal, from the clothing the waiters wore to the salt in the dispenser.

Someone, somewhere has made a successful business out of waiter clothing and someone else is definitely a 'table salt millionaire'. Every hour of every day, I was either reading to increase my business knowledge, my self-confidence or my personal development, or I was coming up with new business ideas. I was so confident that I would be OK, I even spent the last of our savings on a Mediterranean cruise with Amber and my new in-laws. A good friend had received an offer through their work of 90% off a Mediterranean cruise and had kindly shared the offer with us. It emptied my bank account, but I knew if I burned the boats I would have no choice but to come up with something that would work.

It was while driving from Woking to Sutton to pick up Amelia that it occurred. I remember I was coming off the A3 at Tolworth and stuck in some traffic. It was a hot day and my radio was playing up. Because I am a grown adult, I decided to fix the radio by poking it with all my fingers in turn, like a drunk piano player. It fixed the radio sound, but it was now flicking through stations of its own accord. It settled on a talk radio programme I would never normally listen to and they were discussing family mediation. A lawyer was incensed that the government were stopping legal aid for legal fees with a solicitor, but was keeping legal aid available for family mediation. My ears pricked up.

It further transpired that they were concerned that it was going to become compulsory to at least consider family mediation before applying to court for a financial or child arrangements order. In one of the books I had read, Duncan Bannatyne's *Anyone Can Do It*, the author mentioned the benefit of responding to any governmental changes or dictates. Duncan had become wealthy by selling up an ice-cream van business and starting a care home for the elderly. He had done this because, at the time, there was a shortage of care homes so the government promised to pay for any empty rooms in new homes built. It was a no-brainer. Duncan risked everything and mortgaged himself to the hilt to build a new care home business, which he would go on to sell for £20 million. *This could be my Duncan Bannatyne moment*, I thought.

I researched the industry and felt I had what it would take to become a family mediator. I had learnt many skills during my police days related to helping disputing couples, neighbours and families. I knew, if I could talk openly and easily with a victim of rape, that I could talk to people going through a divorce. Plus, I had the added life experience of going through a divorce myself and sorting out child arrangements for my daughter. It was perfect. Perfect, except for the fact I had no experience of the industry and absolutely no money.

I decided to sign up for a diploma course in mediation. I put it on my credit card and, after six weeks of study, I had a diploma in mediation services from the Blackwood Institute.

I approached several existing family mediation services, to see if they would let me sit in to gain some experience. I went for services away from where I was based, so they did not feel they were helping a competitor. One such service, based in Fulham, kindly allowed me to sit in with them for the day. It was an eye-opening experience.

The building was old and like a rabbit warren, with no reception or waiting area. The mediator, who was charging his clients back then £300 per session, was also taking new enquiries and administration calls *during* the meetings with clients. It was shocking to see. Clients coming into the building were left to wander around on their own. The mediation sessions themselves were more about feelings and less about resolving the issues the clients wanted to resolve. I just knew I could do better than this. I also wanted to operate mediation online, so I didn't have to get an office. I left that day, having sat through ten hours of mediation, fully confident that not only could I do the job, I could also do it better than the existing providers.

I had read that to set up a name for a business, you should explain what you do in the title. This makes it easier for Google to recognise what you do, so people searching for this service can find you easier. I was setting up a mediation service in Surrey. I knew the website domain was available as I had just bought it and I felt it summed up precisely what we were about. I couldn't afford a fancy logo, so I copied one from another website based overseas with a badge 'SMS' … and Surrey Mediation Service was born.

My first office was a cupboard under the stairs. I had a laptop, a printer and a load of positive energy. I couldn't afford to have the website developed, so I built it myself using a web-building template. I couldn't afford a professional email account, so I used Zoho email as I thought it looked better than using a Gmail account. I set up a '0330' number as I didn't want to look amateurish and use a mobile number. I launched the rather terrible website, set up some even more terrible Google ads and waited for the phone to ring. It was October 2011. Oh, and to add to the pressure of making sure the business worked, Amber was pregnant.

I had no office and couldn't afford to rent one, so when I got my first clients, I had to kick Amber, the kids and our dog, Stormie, out of the house on a long walk until the coast was clear. I used what I had learnt on my diploma, my experience of working in the police and the ten hours' experience of witnessing other mediators working. And I discovered something of a pleasant surprise: I was actually quite good at mediation.

As a new business, I wanted as many clients as possible, so I made myself available to offer mediation seven days per week and would mediate up to 9 pm in the evening. Where possible, I would drive to the clients' houses for the mediation, as it meant I didn't have to pay out for a meeting room. Eventually, I managed to hire a meeting room at an office near me and then went on to commit to a small one-person office on a monthly basis.

I was taking on *any* type of mediation at this stage. I was travelling to people's gardens to measure hedges in neighbour disputes. I was visiting companies to resolve disputes between staff members. I helped education facilities with student and teacher disputes. I was happy to go anywhere and see anyone and help mediate on absolutely anything. In the first month of trading, I turned over £600, which at the time was a massive boost to me.

But because of all the motivational reading I had done, because I knew I wanted to run a successful business, not just work in my own business and because I knew that I would not be able to meet my three goals if I simply ran a local mediation service based in Surrey, I decided, in January 2012, three months after I went live with Surrey Mediation Service, to buy the domain name MediateUK. *Just in case*, I thought.

The first few months of the business were busy. I had a good flow of clients and new enquiries. I got a few good systems in place for the mediation service and was helping people reach an agreement. Based on forecast figures, I reckoned I could have continued down this route and perhaps, eventually, earned a good annual salary of £30,000 to £40,000 per year. But that wasn't going to align with my goals. It wouldn't have bought us a house in Surrey, big enough for all the children. It wouldn't have been me running a successful business, instead it would have been me working for myself. And I knew that, when you work for yourself, the boss is usually a complete idiot! I also knew it would not net me the £22 million net worth that I had committed to. So I decided to expand.

It was at a friend's grandfather's funeral that I first approached Ian – another good friend from the rugby club. Ian had been the chairman of the rugby club and ran his own advertising agency in London. When I had separated from Karena, Ian and his wife, who was also called Ali, put me up in their home for a few months and refused to charge me a penny in rent for doing so. Their kindness allowed me to be near Amelia, who had moved back to Sutton with her mum, and they even let Amelia stay over for the night. They were ridiculously generous to me at a highly emotive and difficult time in my life.

Living with them also showed me what a good marriage should look like. I had never really seen that before. Despite being together for many years, they were still madly in love with one another and treated each other with respect and dignity. They made decisions together and took into account the other person's viewpoint. They just worked as a couple. And in all my life, I hadn't really seen that up close before. *THIS is what a marriage should look like*, I thought.

I wanted to find a way to repay Ian for the kindness he had shown me at the time of my separation. On hearing that his advertising business was struggling and he was looking for other incomes, I invited him to come on board as a family mediator.

Ian agreed he would like to look into it. He spent a few months shadowing me at various mediation sessions, before committing to come on board and he underwent the family mediation foundation course. I had no idea at the time that, some ten years later, he would become one of the best mediators in the whole country and achieve the top rating as a mediator supervisor, called a PPC. He would become the main trainer and guide for all our mediators at Mediate UK and be absolute key to the growth and progression of the business as it progressed to become the largest private family mediation service in the UK.

Ian's background in advertising meant I had an additional resource to turn to on matters of progressing the business. Having run his own business for many years, I think Ian had a different approach to expansion. I wanted to grow a national business that would meet my goals for myself and my family. Ian preferred to work *in* a business. They are different skills and require a different outlook and mindset. But it didn't matter at this stage, as we had just ourselves and another mediator, Lorraine, who was also a social worker, so she had a good background for family mediation as well.

Caroline then joined us as she had also taken a family mediation course. She was due to set up our third branch, in Islington, North London. I felt good. We had three mediators being trained up, two branches, and I was about to break into London. I had also just become a dad to Dexter, in June 2012. Life was finally working in my favour and I felt happy. I should have known, based on my experiences to date, that it wouldn't last.

Despite following the same marketing strategy for Islington as I had done for our first two branches, in Woking and

Wallington, I could not get the same level of interest in our London branch. I was draining money on a small office in Islington that was lying empty and I had invested thousands in Google advertising to try and get interest going. None of it worked and everything I tried failed. With no money left in the business, I had to sell my flat in order to tide us over. My goal of buying us a house had just taken a large step backwards.

Having got some money from the sale of the flat, I had another issue now. I had enough money to tide us over, but I had a reduced income as I was not receiving any rent. I knew I had to use the money to invest in the business in order to increase the turnover, so I could afford to live. I heard another service was advertising on the radio and I thought, *if it works for them, then I will do that*. I therefore invested £4,000 in a radio commercial on the local radio station. It completely flopped.

The radio commercial idea was simple. Loads of local people would hear about us and click on our website. The trouble was, our website was not ranking highly on Google – I hadn't really heard of Search Engine Optimisation (SEO) at this stage of my business career. So instead people would click on our Google ads, meaning I paid thousands for people to hear about us, thousands of pounds for people to click on our online advert and, even then, as the radio commercial only ran for six weeks, we saw little return on our investment.

With no money left to invest in the business and my ego severely deflated from Islington's failure to get any traction, I focused my attention on trying to improve what we had.

With costs becoming an issue, I had to let Lorraine know we wouldn't have enough work to keep her on. We were back to just Ian and myself. We decided to focus purely on family mediation. Ian, as a trained mediator, did the mediating and I did the admin, marketing and business. It was a good partnership and worked well. But it was a job – and I really didn't want a job. I knew that all jobs I had done had ended in disaster, as I was not doing what I wanted to do. I wanted to grow a great business, not be running a good, but small and local, family mediation service.

One of my earlier clients was an interesting couple to mediate with. Individually they were lovely. They were friendly, professional and kind. Throw them in a room together and they changed in an instant. They just couldn't get on and were, quite correctly in my opinion, getting a divorce. The issue was: they had a 10-year-old daughter, who they both clearly adored, but could not agree on how best to parent her. As a dentist, one of the clients was keen for their daughter to never eat sweets. So when she came home from staying with her dad, there would always be empty sweet wrappers in her pocket. He did it to wind her up. She would then retaliate by denying contact with their daughter. It was a mess. They couldn't even agree on which photos each of them would keep of their daughter. Slowly and patiently, over eight mediation sessions, we managed to help them reach a full agreement on finances and child arrangements. The relief in the room was tangible. We were almost high-fiving each other! I drafted their paperwork and sent it to them to have made into a legally binding agreement by their solicitor.

A few months later, the husband contacted me again. He said his solicitor had charged him over £3,000 in fees and was trying to undo the agreement they had reached through mediation and had both been happy with. He asked if he could use *us* to draft the legal paperwork. I explained that we couldn't do that, but as I was still at the stage of doing anything and everything I could think of to try and get money coming into the business, I then set up the UK's first fixed fee mediation and legal packages.

Not only could you reach an agreement through us now, but you could also have it turned into a divorce, separation agreement or financial consent order – and all for a fixed fee.

I also joined up with as many other businesses as I could to try and help clients. I set up an arrangement with a will writing service, financial advisors, estate agents, insurance companies – everything you may need when going through a divorce or separation. We had a great USP, a great mediator in Ian and a desire for constant improvement. So when we were approached by Chloe, who was a family mediator and also a non-practising solicitor, who wanted to work with us, we agreed to her proposal and set up two new branches in Portsmouth and Aldershot.

It was towards the end of 2013 and the business was doing OK. Not well, but we had a steady stream of new and existing clients. Unfortunately, I had some pressing issues at home to contend with.

I was driving on the A3, just past where I had first got the idea for the mediation business, when I received a phone call. It was child services in Sutton. They were calling to let me know that my daughter Amelia, had been placed on a child at risk register. My ex-wife had tried to take her own life by connecting the exhaust from her car through the window, taping it up and, long story short, would have died, had it not been for the fact the car was an eco-model and the fumes would never likely have killed her. The police were called and had to smash the window and she was subsequently sectioned.

This kickstarted a horrific period of dealing with child services and my ex-wife. Amelia came and lived with us in

Woking for a little while. That part was great for me. She already had her own room that we had built and the two boys were sharing a larger room. Dexter was sleeping in our room, so it was a little cramped to say the least. I needed us to move to a larger house. I knew I couldn't buy anywhere, but stood a chance of renting if we moved away from the area.

At the same time, Bailey's paternal father had turned up at our house out of the blue. Bailey's biological father had not seen Bailey since he was a young boy and had certainly shown no interest for many years. Slightly drunk and high on cocaine, he suddenly arrived at our door, demanding to see 'my boy'. I was away at work, but I know the untimely and irresponsible visit further impacted negatively on Bailey's wellbeing.

We started looking for houses to rent and settled on a place near Cardiff, in a little village called Pentyrch. The reasoning was simple. We wouldn't have any sudden visits from absent fathers intent on causing emotional harm to their children; we could give the children a bedroom of their own each; I could run the business remotely and I felt that Cardiff was a good area to set up Divorce Friend – a new business idea I had, to complement the family mediation service. With property prices cheaper in South Wales, I also stood a better chance of buying a house – cheating my goals, I know, but who's checking?

In April 2014, shortly after my fortieth birthday, we packed up and headed to Cardiff for a fresh start and, I hoped, a big jump towards achieving my three main goals in life.

What I didn't know was that the move would mark the start of one of the most difficult periods in my life and push me to do the one thing I never thought I would have to do…. I would be forced to abandon my family.

'There should be no boundaries to human endeavour. We are all different. However bad life may seem, there is always something you can do, and succeed at. While there's life, there is hope.'

— Stephen Hawking

9

I'LL BE THERE NOW, IN A MINUTE. THE WELSH YEARS.

Starting the business and putting most purchases on credit cards, meant my credit score was pretty much shrivelled to nothing. So when we moved, we set up the tenancy agreement through the business and paid six months upfront. The tenancy agreement stated that we would then pay monthly but, at the end of the initial six months, the landlord requested another six months upfront. We didn't have it. We had to up and leave after just six months in the house and move to another property. Then, after another six months, we moved house again.

During this time, I set up a business called Divorce Friend. With help from Business Wales, I was allocated a business mentor and the plan was to use all the existing family mediators in the UK to sell our fixed fee divorce and legal packages. I spent months driving round trying to get other family mediators on board. They all loved the idea, but none of them ended up giving us any referrals. Most had their own set-up with local solicitors and were focused on the family mediation part of their business. The idea of getting paid commission for referrals seemed almost dirty to many of them.

I flipped the business and, this time, set up a direct-to-client offering. All could be done online and we would offer fixed fee divorce and negotiation meetings, barrister reviews, legal advice and referrals to other services. My brother-in-law, Dominic, built a great-looking website and I started to promote it. I was very close to getting funding from an angel investor for £250,000. I was on the verge of something really good, again.

But try as I may, I just couldn't get it to take off. I didn't have the marketing budget to promote nationally, I was offering several new services which clients were not searching for, even though I believed they were better than existing options. Allied to this, two huge issues came up.

In 2015, the mediation industry was generally suffering and many well-established services folded. Surrey Mediation Service was no different, but we did manage to hang in there although our revenue dropped considerably. Each month I would dread coming up to pay day. I stopped paying myself to keep the business liquid and we were reliant on housing benefit and other handouts to stay in our home. Amber had already declared herself bankrupt – albeit under the lesser Debt Relief Order – and I had already sold my other flat and put all of that money into the business, just to try and keep it afloat.

I took out a business loan of £25,000, with a personal guarantee, to help kickstart Divorce Friend, and at one point I was over £50,000 in personal debt, having also put £50,000 from the sale of my flats into the business. Instead of heading towards my £22 million net worth goal, I was minus £100,000 down. I'd have been substantially better off had I not done anything for the past four years! No matter how hard I tried, I couldn't get Divorce Friend to take off and Surrey Mediation Service was struggling along, barely turning over enough to keep going. By paying myself nothing and reducing overheads where I could, including doing all the marketing, accounting and company admin myself, I ended up working twelve-hour days and I worked virtually every weekend. I managed to keep the business afloat – just.

My own health was struggling. I wasn't sleeping well. I was permanently stressed. I thought I would have to lay off our office manager and, meanwhile, she was appalled that I wasn't paying her what she thought she deserved.

Added to this mix of emotional stress and pressure, Amelia had started to complain about coming down to stay with us. She had been put on the child at risk register during her mum's period of deteriorating mental health and we had a social worker visit us in Wales to check our living situation was acceptable. It was soul-destroying trying to answer questions like: 'Why is there an office printer in Amelia's room?'; 'Show me proof that Amelia is happy here?'; 'Have you been violent to her mother recently?'

I would drive up to Sutton from Cardiff to go to meetings with what was usually a different social worker on each occasion. Sometimes I would make the 350-mile round trip drive, only to be told the meeting had been cancelled. Other times, I was asked if I could sit in a room with Amelia's stepdad without being violent to him! Another time they discussed if Amelia was safe with my own children – as they had talked about 'Tea-bagging' (a move they had all learnt from *Call of Duty*). They were clearly being fed a host of lies about me and my family. Eventually I asked for a subject access request, and the report, while poorly redacted showed that Karena had persuaded social services that me – and in particular my relationship with Karena – was the main cause of Amelia's welfare concerns. While going into details about Karena's behaviour as a mother, which didn't exactly reflect well on her, it was clear from the report that Karena and her family blamed me for everything bad in Amelia's life and had tried to paint me in the worst possible light. Nothing could have been further from the truth and matters were to get even worse.

One visit at Christmas with us, Amelia told us she wanted to go home and we had to hastily arrange for her to return back to Surrey. On another visit she cried continually. Eventually Amelia, at just twelve years of age, made the decision that she never wanted to see any of us ever again. She told her mum that I had hit her, which, as anyone who knows me would testify, I could never do. I adored Amelia. I would rather punch myself in the face than hurt her.

The last time she came to stay with us, we kept ourselves busy with a pony ride, we then went to buy popcorn and to get a DVD to watch together. On returning to the house, Amelia started crying uncontrollably in her bed. She said she wanted to go home and she tried to run out of the house with no shoes on. I called her mum and arranged to meet halfway up the M4. I told Amelia on the way home that I loved her, and that all I had ever done was to love her. She stayed silent the whole way. When I handed her over to her mum at the car park of the services near Reading, I didn't know it at the time, but I would not see Amelia ever again.

My heart was destroyed. I could handle being abandoned by my father I grew up with and even, with help, by my real father. But my own daughter? Amelia had been one of my reasons for existing. She had helped me out of my earlier depression, just by being born. I wanted to be a success for her and for Bailey, Dempsey and Dexter. I wanted to provide for them all. I felt like someone had cut out a part of me. I just wasn't the same person after. I was incomplete. A lesser person, just going through the motions of life. Pretending everything was fine. I was surviving, not living.

Around the same time as this, Bailey was getting in trouble at school and had to have talks with the fire brigade for trying to set fire to our small Welsh village(!) and Dexter ... well, Dexter was struggling, to say the least.

We didn't know about autism at the time. We just knew that we would get two-to-three calls each day throughout his nursery, pre-school and then reception, stating they had needed to remove the other children from the area, as Dexter was causing a 'disturbance'. This disturbance may be trashing the whole classroom, punching, kicking or hitting other children and nursery workers or generally being difficult. His behaviour at home was not much better. Amber's full-time role at this stage was to try and maintain as much a sense of normality as possible. Looking after Dexter was a full-time job and Amber did it admirably.

Five years later, Dexter would not only have managed to stay within the mainstream school system, against all odds, he would also have grown into a boy who is kind, curious, loving and incredibly funny. His autism is simply part of who he is. It's a gift that makes him wonderful. We now know how to better support him and received the most wonderful guidance from his primary school in Rugby. Dexter is an absolute joy to us. I am so proud of him. Amber deserves a huge amount of credit for her patience and support in raising him.

If I am being honest, we struggled to settle and fit in, in Wales. We were English – and having an autistic child, who has probably already hit any potential new friends' own little darling, doesn't help when it comes to getting invited to social gatherings. Plus, I was working all the time. I was juggling trying to get Divorce Friend up and running successfully, trying to keep Surrey Mediation Service from failing and trying to be the father I aspired to.

I didn't realise it, but I was in freefall and heading towards a complete burnout. I was self-medicating by drinking a bottle of wine most evenings. I would usually pass out on the sofa and wake up in the morning dehydrated and tired. I'd spend my working day trying to put out fires at work, keeping the plates spinning and trying to get enough money coming in to pay all the invoices. Most of our household bills were put on credit cards.

I was desperate to keep up this façade that everything was OK. Rather than get help, or be honest and open up to anyone, I made out that things were fine. I didn't want them to see me for what I was: a shell of the person I wanted to be; a failure at business and a failure as a father to my daughter. If people could see the real me, they would surely *all* desert me and then I would have no one? *No.* I had to keep up pretences that all was OK and the business was doing fine.

As we entered the second half of 2017, the financial situation was so desperate that, if we hadn't received a £1,000 commission from a supplier one week, we would have gone under the next day. The stress of wondering if we would fail, if I would have to pick up the phone to Ian or Hannah and tell them that I couldn't afford to pay them, or to fold the business that had consumed every part of my life for the last five years, was intolerable. Something had to give.

I would get through to Friday each week, having managed to not collapse the business and I'd drink a bottle of wine. Amber would go to bed and I would stay up, sometimes opening – and even finishing – a second bottle of wine. I'd punish myself by playing clips from YouTube of daughters and fathers having good times together. I'd play the scene from *The Patriot* where Mel Gibson's character's daughter runs after him: 'Father, father, I'll say anything.' I'd listen to songs about daughters and fathers. I'd think about how I could possibly turn the business around. How I could ever be a success and how far away I was from getting there. I'd Google mental health charities or 'how to kill yourself painlessly', and I would cry for hours, sat in the dark on my own. I'd cover my face with a cushion to reduce any sounds I made, desperate not to wake Amber or the boys up. If she knew, she would surely leave me too.

My depression was so intense that I genuinely believed I was toxic to my family, to my friends and to my business. It must be all my fault, surely? I knew my natural parents were both intelligent and successful people – so what was wrong with me? I became convinced that my family would be better off without me. Any moments of joy would be quickly clouded by feelings of angst and despair. I felt I was the business and its failing was a direct reflection of how awful I was as a human being. I felt on edge all the time. Anxious, worried and highly stressed. My weight grew, and I had issues with my liver from drinking too much, meaning the level of ferritin in my blood was three times the absolute maximum it should be for a man of my age. These excess levels of iron, brought on by liver damage, leads to extreme tiredness. And that isn't great when you are not sleeping due to stress and need a clear head to try and work out how to save your business.

A low point for me at this time came with a phone call I received from Amber. She was in floods of tears. I asked her whatever was the matter and she explained her credit card had just been declined at Asda, when doing the weekly food shop. Amber was familiar, at this difficult stage in our lives, with her debit card being declined, but her backup was always her credit card. She had now reached – and exceeded – the credit limit. I said I would drive up to meet her and pay. But not before I collapsed to the ground in despair. This was my role in life. Surely an absolute minimum requirement, as a father, is to provide for my family? Now, I couldn't even afford to feed mine. I managed to find three credit cards and drove to Asda, where I had to split the shopping bill between them all at the customer service desk. It was embarrassing, humbling and completely soul-destroying. I had to take action and do something to change this – and quickly. The food we had purchased would only last us another week after all...

It was clear the business could not continue to support paying Hannah, Ian and myself. So I made one of the worst decisions, in the history of bad decisions, since the captain of the Titanic decided the icebergs really weren't an issue. I decided that *I* should be the one who should go.

I called a team meeting and explained that I was leaving working in the business full-time as I had got myself a job. I explained I would still be involved in the marketing but that times were too difficult for me to continue. I followed it up with an email explaining my reasons and how the business was struggling. I asked Hannah if she would like to increase her hours from six to eight. She gave me a look as though I had just asked her if she would like me to piss on her cornflakes. Her mother had recently passed away and my asking her this question at that time was, in her opinion, insensitive to the extreme. *I only want to pay you more money, like you have been constantly banging on about!* I thought. But I didn't say that; I was too weak minded and down on myself. I just took her views on board and apologised for being so insensitive.

'I'll rise like the day. I'll rise up. I'll rise unafraid. I'll rise up. And I'll do it a thousand times again'

— Andra Day

10

SENT TO COVENTRY

The job I had managed to hastily get myself was working for the Financial Ombudsman Service (FOS) in their newly opened office in Coventry.

As a contractor, the pay was good. I would have a monthly income that would allow me, finally, to have some financial options. The downside to it was that I would have to spend the working week in Coventry and leave behind my family in Wales. It also meant I couldn't work full time for Surrey Mediation Service and I was worried that it would fold. Also, as a contractor, the amount of money I had left over each month, after paying various taxes plus my accommodation and travel expenses, was not great. But it was the only way I could see myself getting out of the situation I had gotten my family into.

This decision also meant that I had to work away and miss Amber's 40th birthday, which she spent eating a takeaway curry by herself. I don't think I can ever forgive myself for that.

I think Ian and Hannah were quite happy with the fact I was leaving. My constant attempts to build and grow the business were exhausting for them. They just wanted to do a day's work and get paid – and who could blame them? They now had the run of the ship and freedom to work together, without my interference.

My accommodation in Coventry was a room on the ground floor of a modern town house. Also in the accommodation were two Chinese students studying at Coventry University and a guy who worked for Jaguar Land Rover, who are based nearby. My first week at FOS was awful. I was ill, having caught a bad cold, and the training was difficult and challenging. I also missed my family terribly. I have learnt that I just don't operate as well without them beside me. Even if I am working in my office at home, hearing their screams, arguments, chats and the general family buzz keeps me going. As one of my six pillars of support, they are, after all, the main purpose of what I am working for.

On the way home after my first week, I was feeling so ill, having to stand most of the way on a packed train and regretting my decision already, that when I was collected by Amber and Dexter from Cardiff train station, I just broke down in tears.

The Financial Ombudsman Service deals with complaints about its member organisations. These are mostly banks, insurance companies and other financial services. With PPC claims going through the roof they had a massive backlog of work and needed to do something drastic about it. They hired a couple of hundred contractors and our job was to evaluate a PPC claim, after the financial body had rejected it and see if it would be upheld. Most of the complaints are not, but some were.

The issue was that, not only were the systems that had been put in place originally not suitable for the massive flood of complaints FOS received about PPC, each company, sub company, financial product and set of circumstances of the person complaining would have different outcomes. The terms and conditions would change on a regular basis and you could be dealing with a complaint over thirty years old. For someone of average intelligence such as myself, it was extremely challenging.

FOS had a traffic light system for scoring your work. Green was all good, with few if any minor mistakes. Amber was ok, but usually there would be many minor mistakes or a more serious but recoverable one. Red was a serious error, which could have impacted the outcome of the complaint or impacted negatively on FOS.

If you got three reds in a row, you were summoned into a meeting room and dismissed on the spot. The culture within the company was one of the worst I have ever witnessed. You would return to your desk from a coffee break to find that the person sitting next to you had been turfed out and there was just a blank desk waiting to be filled by another unfortunate soul.

To get through the probation, you had to complete twelve cases at a rate of one case per week. My first two cases were both red. One more and I would be gone. My next six were all amber cases. I was hanging on by the skin of my teeth. I finally got a green and then another green, and managed to get through to the New Year and be accepted as accredited. The reward for such an achievement is a quadrupling of your caseload.

I would often work from 9 am until 9 pm and then return back to my room in the bedsit, eat a cold pizza left over from the previous night and spend a couple of hours working on Surrey Mediation Service. I didn't mind the working hours as I had little else to do and being busy kept my mind from wandering to my family, still in Wales, without me.

But it was a dire existence. My contract was for a maximum
of two years. I thought I may be able to get a permanent role
there some day and my manager was a genuinely affable chap,
who seemed to like me. In such difficult working circumstances,
I became the 'dad' of our group. And I was looked after in this
role by the 'mum' of the group, Ania. Ania is from Poland and
a mum to two (lovely) children. She was desperate to buy a
house herself and we just got on and worked well together. She
helped me with my cases, as she was far better than I was at the
work, whilst feeding me healthy treats and snacks. In return, I
made her laugh and helped her with her cases where I could. We
formed a little team around us and everyone supported each
other. It is often when faced with extreme situations like the one
we were working in, that people can really pull together and the
abiding memory I have from my time at FOS was of the people,
busy working away to try to reach their own weekly target
(otherwise they might get sacked) but also giving up that
precious time to help others with their cases.

Surrounded by supportive Sally's, people such as Ania,
helped me get through my time at FOS. I have no doubt that I
would have been dismissed, had it not been for her support.

The bedsit I was staying at was not exactly working out well.
One of the Chinese students had become accustomed to using
my allocated shower room to do her necessaries in. One
morning I was happily flicking through my phone, while seated
on the toilet, and I happened to glance over to my right to see
her used panty liner resting menacingly on the radiator. It was
like slowing down for a road accident; I didn't want to look, but
couldn't help it.

For a whole week, this piece of damaged cloth got crustier
and curlier on the radiator. It was only when I found a new, fresh

one lying next to it that I held my breath and found the courage to remove them to the bin. In the best passive-aggressive nature of living with housemates, I taped a notice above the radiator: 'Please don't leave your used sanitary products here. You wrong uns'. I don't know if it was related, but neither Chinese student returned to the house the following week. This was good news for the landlord, as they would keep the thermostat turned up to a tropical twenty-eight degrees centigrade, and then, when it inevitably got too hot, would simply open the windows to cool down.

My happiness at the Chinese students going was short-lived. In their place, I had an overweight builder, who wanted the room next to me on the ground floor. I no longer had the floor to myself and, more importantly, we had to share the tiny bathroom and toilet. I'm going to call the builder Charlie, although we never officially met. Our hours did not coincide at all and by the time I got home from the day at FOS, Charlie was busy on his third or fourth beer. Charlie loved beer. He also loved burping loudly after a beer and watching TV on high volume late into the evening. Sometimes Charlie liked to treat himself to a good old-fashioned wank, which, with the walls about as thin as a footballer's wife, I could hear in full surround sound. Whatever activity he felt like doing in an evening, he always made sure he finished up by falling asleep and snoring so loudly I thought he was in bed next to me (which, given his taste in porn, I really didn't want).

I left the bedsit soon after and moved into a house with another friend from FOS. That was enjoyable, but I needed my family around me and Amber agreed to move up to the area so we could have yet another fresh start.

Still determined to buy a house, we thought the Midlands would allow us to do that more easily, especially as I was now earning a decent monthly wage. And if I could get Surrey Mediation Service working better, I may even be able to get a passive income from that as well. Amber found us a property in a town called Lutterworth and we moved there. I continued to commute to Coventry each day and, for a very short period of time, we felt like a 'normal family'. But, as you may have gathered from reading this far, we are far from normal – and I soon made another terrible decision. I left working at the Financial Ombudsman Service and took up another job as a business development manager for a local subprime mortgage broker.

It was a self-employed position and I thought the job was to help develop the business and help the managing director out. What the actual job entailed was cold calling businesses and getting referrals from them. It was horrific for me. I got rejection after rejection – and we all know how I handle rejection by now, don't we? I lasted just two weeks and I used a prostate cancer scare (all clear now, no issues) as my excuse to leave.

It was during my prostate cancer scare that the doctor offered me some Viagra.

I'll have some of that! I thought, and I got a few months' worth.

Even Amber took some to see what effect, if any, it had! The rest were put aside and would reappear just under a year later during that unfortunate Travelodge incident.

'You miss 100% of the shots you don't take'

– Wayne Gretzky

11

THE FINAL COUNTDOWN

I was already seeing a counsellor locally, as I was struggling with life at that time. I had no career, no successful business to speak of. Having left FOS and the business development job, we had no income again. I had moved my whole family for a fresh start and felt I was in an even worse place than before. My counsellor asked me what I wanted to do and I told her: I felt I needed to make Surrey Mediation Service a success. I had put so much of my life into it.

With her guidance and advice, I decided to return to Surrey Mediation Service and turn it into the business I had wanted it to be when I first envisaged it. I would grow it into a fantastic business, covering the whole of the UK. I would use the website – Mediate UK – that I had kept all these years, and we would expand and grow into something I could be proud of and something that would not give me sleepless nights and endless pressure. I would do things right this time, get help when I needed it and use the right people at the right time. I would run the business as I had read about in all those business books.

I didn't know it then, but my decision to return to Surrey Mediation Service that day, taken in a Waitrose café ('cos, as my mum said, I'm upper middle class!) and following that consultation with my counsellor, would almost kill me …

It was June 2018 and I was excited. Amber had agreed to join me for the trip to Woking and she would see her old friends, while I held a meeting with Ian, Hannah and Chloe about my return to the business; my plans for growth and expansion and my vision on what we needed to do – and do differently – to make it really work. I needed their buy-in and I was pumped at the opportunity I now had to revive the business.

The meeting was, without a doubt, one of the worst experiences of my life. My revelation that I was returning to the company went down like a fart in a busy lift. Ian was livid. How dare I spring such a thing on them without any warning?

During the meeting, I congratulated Hannah on how many calls the phone stats showed she had taken over the past couple of months. Her response was that it was completely unacceptable that I was monitoring the number of calls she took. I mean, it's not like I am trying to run a business, is it? Every suggestion I made was treated with a rebuke or just contempt. It was horrible. I suggested we needed to sell some of the vouchers for online wills that were sitting on the company's books. Ian argued that no one would want these as they would prefer to go to a solicitor. I explained the opportunity available for our divorce facilitation packages (as they are now called) and was told by Ian and Chloe that they no longer wished to do these as they weren't considered mediation. Every suggestion I made was shot down. We closed the meeting and I was devastated. I felt I had just been rejected by the very business that I had set up. My return was not wanted and certainly not welcomed. Ian would be absolutely devastated to hear that I felt bullied.

What they didn't know was that the business was unfortunately not operating any better in my absence. It was still just ambling along and we were not making a profit, even without the expenses or income that I incurred. I had sold two flats, worked seven-day weeks, twelve-hour days. I had lived, breathed and devoted all my attention into Surrey Mediation Service. And now I felt like I was being treated as an annoyance, an unwelcome and meddling nuisance. I had nothing left. Still, I had some good news for Hannah. My return meant that she no longer needed to work the eight hours she had taken on a few months prior and which had caused such an issue for her at the time.

I told her that she could return to six hours now and that I hoped that came as good news. It didn't. Hannah's face screwed up in front of me and she spouted a whole blurb of vitriolic anger. How dare I treat people like this? How dare I change her hours again? How dare I monitor how much work she does? How dare I pay her just 33% *over* the minimum wage? It was horrific. Any sane person would have calmly and politely thanked her for her work to date, explained that it was unacceptable to speak to the person who pays you as she had just done, and calmly told her to "fuck off". But I was definitely *not* a sane person. I simply apologised once again and told her I would review it at a later date. I was about as far from being a leader in my business as it was possible to be.

Amber and I had booked dinner and a night at a nearby hotel through a Groupon offer. We were due to meet some old friends. I explained how horrific the meeting had been and how Hannah had spoken to me, as I got into the car. Amber wanted to pull over there and then and go back to have a word with Hannah herself. I don't think I had ever seen her so angry. But

I managed to dissuade her from doing so. We drove to the hotel and I called Chloe. Maybe I had got it all wrong and I had come across as a complete tyrant? Chloe confirmed that I hadn't and seemed shocked that I was calling to check. She could sense there was some tension at the meeting, but didn't feel it was down to me. But I took it as being completely down to me!

I undressed and got into the shower. The water was pounding on my head and I kept thinking, *what have I done so wrong to upset Ian and Hannah so much? I thought they would welcome me back.* All the stresses and tensions from the previous six years imploded in me, and I had what I now know to be a fully blown panic attack. Amber found me curled up in a ball, in the corner of the bathroom, shower still raining down on me, crying uncontrollably as I cradled my knees and rocked back and forth against the wall. I'd finally had the physical breakdown to accompany my ongoing mental breakdown. I'd reverted to being a small child.

If there is one thing that Amber is good at, it's being my cheerleader. She has maintained faith in me even through every awful event, every forced house move, every red letter bill we couldn't pay, even dealing with bailiffs turning up at the door. She did this all while raising three boys, one of whom is now diagnosed with autism and needed constant care and attention. If Amber had not come on that trip, I have no doubt I would not be here now. My body had given up, my heart was making palpitations, my brain had degenerated to that of a child. Amber took hold of me, told me how proud she was of me and, within just an hour, was making me laugh and sharing a drink with me. She is amazing.

As part of my decision to 'do things properly', I had decided to get some outside help and employ a mentor or business coach. I also fessed up to Ian and Hannah that my mental health was not great. I underplayed it still, but for the first time in my life I had confessed to someone else that I was struggling mentally. Ian responded exactly as I thought he would. He gave me a break, listened to me, showed compassion and kindness. He sent me a gift box of retro sweets to enjoy and spoke to me at length about mental health and his own struggles in this area. He stepped up as a friend. Hannah asked for another pay rise.

Despite this, my relationship with Ian was still difficult. He wrote me an email from the heart, and with genuine good intent, saying how our expansion plans hadn't worked and he couldn't see how they would. We had set up a fourth branch in Caterham and he believed this was a complete waste of time and further sign of me meddling unnecessarily with the business. He said I should have simply taken my family mediation foundation course and I could have set up in Rugby and settled for being a really good family mediator. He was chastising my business decisions, but doing so with warmth and love and, on what I had managed so far, who could blame him? Neither of us had any evidence to the contrary.

But, from my point of view, Ian might as well have written: *See all those dreams and goals you had for your life? You need to forget all that shit about becoming a successful businessman and concentrate on having a proper job to support your family like normal people do.* His advice came from a kind and loving place, but it just made me feel even worse about myself.

If my relationship with Ian was strained at this point, my relationship with Hannah had deteriorated into a cesspit. I had told her I would be getting a business coach to work with me and that part of their role would be to review the business and how we could afford to pay *everyone* more money. I reminded her that she had only ever had a pay increase, that I was taking nothing from the business and meanwhile Amber had taken on a job as a cleaner to help us make ends meet. This fell on deaf ears. She felt that what I paid her was an insult and told me by continuing to pay her that amount, I was abusing her and our friendship. I was in such a low place that I didn't sack her, even after that ridiculous comment.

I interviewed four business coaches and settled on one, called Sean. Sean explained what he felt he could do for the business. He gave me advice on my debts and came across as though he knew what he was talking about. He gave me some references to check on him and explained he wanted to get me some investment from people he had contacts with. He also said we needed to revisit our business plan and business model and that he had partners who could help with that. Finally, he explained he was happy to work with Ian, Chloe and Hannah to rebuild the morale in the company. It all sounded perfect for what we needed.

I spoke to his references, one of whom was a lawyer, who Sean had helped. I felt confident about him and, being sure I was making the right choice, took him on board. It turns out that Sean was an alcoholic and a blagger at best; a complete conman at worse.

I found it strange that there was no contract to be signed, but I handed him £5,000 … and then another £5,000. To his credit, Sean did do loads of work for me. It was just that he didn't have a clue what he was talking about. He insisted I put magnetic boards on my car, and those of my family and anyone else who worked for us. He spent his days doing business networking at events in areas where we didn't even have a branch offering. But, before I knew he was a fraud, I let him loose on the company.

Sean spoke in depth with Ian, who was his usual helpful self, and I believe Sean did some good in trying to put my views across. He also spoke to Hannah, which went less well. After his first meeting with her, he called me up to say that she had no motivation to stay at Surrey Mediation and no future with the company. I still didn't have the balls to stop using her services.

I was pressing ahead at this stage with Mediate UK and, because Hannah had made clear she didn't get paid enough to do any other work, we were also going to keep Surrey Mediation Service running as a separate entity. It was a ridiculous decision, put in because I wanted to pacify someone I still considered a friend and yet who had no desire or motivation to work for my business. I also had to keep divorce facilitation as a separate business because Hannah, Ian and Chloe didn't want anything to do with it, so I ran that part as a separate company. I had *three* companies, all doing similar things. It was a ridiculous set-up, and only done to try and keep my team happy. The bottom line was I was not managing, or in control of, my own business and that is never a good thing for anyone involved.

We wanted to recruit more mediators and, as Sean was based near Bracknell and had a contact at an accountancy firm, we set up a new head office nearby in a village called Binfield. We also recruited five new mediators to join us, with the intention of setting up four new branches.

Mediate UK was starting to form and a big part of this was getting a new website developed. I spent ages looking at website designs, what worked and what didn't, and I worked with a developer to get one launched. Ian hated it, but by this stage I think I could have launched Amazon and poor Ian would have disliked it!

Sean had not helped with the tensions in the company, as hoped. His advice on finances had been incorrect. The promised investment never materialised. He set me up with an accountant who couldn't work out VAT and, instead of our receiving a VAT payment back of £6,000 as he had assured me, we were faced with a VAT bill of £8,000. The company just could not handle a £14,000 difference in the cash flow.

It also turned out that Sean's method of operation was to get a new business under his wing and then simply persuade any other businesses in his mentor group to take on their services – even when it was not suitable or, as with my case, ridiculously overpriced. He had set me up with an automated software developer that was far more complicated than what we needed at the time. He told me that social media was the way forward and got me into a contract with a new start-up, charging £720 per month to send out a few posts to our social media platforms. As a comparison, I now have better social media posts, with a far superior and more targeted system, for which I pay £300 per month, (thank you Jack at OptiModo).

In March 2019, our turnover plummeted. It was simply not sustainable – I had invested heavily in the new website and in Mediate UK, but this was yet to bear dividends. Meanwhile, Sean and I had just agreed to share the employment of a new member of staff, called Belinda, who would work part-time for us at Mediate UK and part-time on Sean's 'business coaching' service. It was yet another fixed cost, along with the spacious new office in Binfield.

My relationship with Hannah had deteriorated by this stage to an untenable one. She still wanted a pay rise and told me she was happy to work either on a contract basis or as a full-time employee. We asked what her pay demands were and she insisted we double her wages. In addition to this, she had told me that she had no intention of training or helping Belinda progress, would only work on matters to do with Surrey Mediation Service and not Mediate UK or Divorce Friend, and wanted a whole load of other perks and payments completely misaligned with what the role entailed … which was basically answering the phone, responding to emails, invoicing and booking in clients.

In addition to this, I had allowed her to talk to me with disgust and disdain for over six months. I planned my calls with her to include a half-hour 'recovery slot' afterwards, as I knew I would need to go for a lie down to get over the conversation before I could talk to anyone else. It still baffles me why I would ever let anyone treat me that way, let alone pander to them and then pay them to do so. It was all a sign of my rapidly deteriorating mental health. Things were about to come to a short, sharp head.

Unsurprisingly, with Hannah losing all interest in the business, our turnover experienced a rapid decline in February and March 2019, going back to levels not seen for five years prior. But our business costs were significantly up compared to then. One Wednesday, I noticed lots of messages coming through and could see that Hannah had just deserted the job for that afternoon. She still billed me for the four hours she didn't work. The same day, I'd had to cancel Dexter's swimming lessons, as we could no longer afford them. The four hours I paid her for not working would have covered those lessons, almost to the pound. Hannah had basically given up and it reflected in our income.

At the end of March, having offered Hannah a full-time contract, for less money than she wanted, she called up to give us one day's notice that she was leaving. A final kick in the belly from her, meaning we had no cover for the Monday. That weekend was my birthday weekend and we cancelled the celebrations so I could catch up with the admin work that hadn't been completed that week.

Belinda was starting at Binfield on the Monday and I had arranged to stay in the Travelodge at Bracknell for two weeks to train her up. That training was going to be more intense now, as we were going to have to cover for Hannah too. The first week, Belinda and I struggled through. We answered calls and responded to emails as Belinda was literally thrown in at the deep end. I honestly felt she would leave us any day; the situation was so stressful and manic.

I was also struggling at the time with my mum, who was experiencing the early onset of Alzheimer's. A few days into Belinda's first week, I got a call from my mum to say her kitchen ceiling had collapsed and I had to rush to Croydon from my hotel at 6 am to deal with it. Poor Belinda had to cover the phone calls and enquiries on her own, with no training or mediation knowledge. As I would later find out, Belinda, quite typically, just took it in her stride.

Alongside sorting the collapsed ceiling, my stepfather Trevor had required an operation and new hip installed, so he needed additional care. My mum's investment flat in Ewell had been taken over by drug dealers and we had to get the tenants evicted and the whole place refurbished before the police and council seized it from her!

I was working silly hours and juggling too many things; I didn't have enough time for Amber and the boys. Amber was great, as always, and agreed we could miss our anniversary. Ian had by then made the decision that he didn't want to be part of Mediate UK's future and resigned his position. But again, being Ian, he said he wouldn't leave us for at least three months and would fully support me in the handover of all his clients.

I also decided that I would try to do the right thing and send Hannah a bunch of flowers to say 'Thank you' for her work at Surrey Mediation Service. That proved to be another mistake, as it was the final straw for her and she threatened me with legal action. I also received an email from her husband – someone I considered a long-time friend. It read that if I thought a bunch of flowers would make up for the horrific way I had treated his wife, I was very much mistaken. He made no mention of how horrifically Hannah had treated me and my business. I knew, in that instant, that my friendship with him was over and was also likely to affect my friendships with all my friends from the rugby club.

All my pillars of support were collapsing below me at the same time. My mother was about to lose her mind to dementia, my daughter couldn't bear to see or engage with me, I felt both my fathers had rejected me, my friends pillar was crumbling down.

My work pillar had shattered to nothing. I was about to go bust and at the worst possible time, having just taken on new mediators and a new member of staff. And I had spent over £10,000 on a business coach and mentor who was an incompetent fraud. I would later get a call from some of his other associates who were concerned he was trying to dupe other clients and was making inappropriate sexual advances to females in his coaching group. They also confirmed that the days on business planning they spent with me, for which he charged me £1,000, should have been free of charge as they were using it to test drive a new way of working. Sean had just pocketed the money himself. I felt so stupid for trusting him.

The only pillar of support I felt I had left standing was my relationship pillar. This was as strong as ever, except I felt I didn't deserve it. I had absolute certainty in my mind that Amber and my children would be better off without me in their lives. I was crystal clear on that. It was why I didn't reach out to Amber that night, when I was swallowing all those pills and Sauvignon Blanc. It was why I didn't call my sister, who I know would have provided me with all the support I would have needed. Who would want a husband or brother without friends, without an income, without a business and without any hope for the future? It had been eight years since I resigned from the police, and I had nothing to show for it other than £50,000 worth of debt and another £50,000 blown from my properties. The least I could do was let Amber have £250,000 in 'compensation' for her poor judgement in choosing me.

Of course, none of that is remotely near the truth.

My friends *didn't* all hate me. If Hannah was so unhappy in her role at Surrey Mediation, I should have sorted it out with her, or agreed it wasn't going to work and departed happily. I should have done more to understand her issues and why she felt like she did. I should have done more due diligence on Sean and not paid him a penny until we had a proper contract in place. I should have used my own judgement in making business decisions. Mediate UK wasn't dead, it was just down in the dumps and needed reviving. And Hannah's husband was, quite rightly, sticking up for his wife – which I would expect anyone to do. Moreover, Amber's life would have been devastated and so would my children's if I had not survived that night in the

Travelodge. At the time I couldn't see any of this. My brain just wasn't functioning correctly.

I do see it now, with absolute clarity.

I need to share with you, I feel immense guilt. I feel sick writing about this, knowing my children and people I care deeply about will read this. But if sharing my story stops just one person from trying to kill themselves, then sharing all this has got to be worth it. I really hope it pays off.

As I drove to the Binfield office the morning after my suicide attempt, I figured to myself that at least things couldn't get any worse. I must absolutely make sure that the previous evening was my rock bottom and that it would never happen again. I owed that to my family at least. To this day, I have never allowed myself to get that low again. Instead, I utilise the tools I have learnt and share in this book. I let people know if I am struggling. I get help if I need it, at the first sign of trouble, not when it is too late.

That morning, when against the odds, I did wake up, I promised I would smile to the world, be positive and make my business into the one that I had envisioned all those years ago. To this day, I have managed to do just that and it is, in no small part, thanks to someone who had just resigned from the company and a fantastic lady from South Africa, called Belinda.

'What counts in life is not the mere fact that we have lived. It is what difference we have made to the lives of others that will determine the significance of the life we lead.'

— Nelson Mandela

12

A FRIEND, A SAFFA AND A BUSINESS COACH

When I got into the office that morning, Belinda was already in. She greeted me with a smile, made me a coffee and thanked me again for giving her the opportunity of the job. She was so positive, so full of purpose and energy, I allowed myself a glimpse of optimism. Seeing Belinda work so enthusiastically during her first few weeks, even though she had received no proper training and was dumped headfirst into the role, gave me renewed purpose and vigour. Her optimism and willingness to work shone through. It is absolutely no coincidence that turnover increased in Belinda's second month of working with us, by 66%.

Instead of having someone who didn't want to work in the business and certainly didn't want to work for me, I had someone who was happy and also desperate to do well. The difference was palpable.

Belinda's efforts helped turnover get to a level where we could continue the business and the plans we had for Mediate UK started bearing fruit. I sacked Sean – who would later try to sue me for £18,000, which was quite frankly thought up in cloud-cuckoo-land. I also stopped using everyone who he had recommended to me. I took advantage of a break clause after three months with the social media company, to stop using their overpriced and not particularly great service and then they also tried, unsuccessfully, to sue me!

The biggest impact on the business's future success was an unexpected but delightful surprise – we got Ian back.

When my mum's ceiling collapsed, I had called Ian and asked for his help with assisting Belinda. He had responded exactly as expected and dropped everything to help out. He later told me that this made him realise that he still cared and cared deeply about me and the business. I was waiting to see some potential clients at our Woking office one evening, when he phoned me up. 'Trigg, will you consider keeping me on at Mediate UK?'

I didn't hesitate for a second. I'm not sure I even let him finish the sentence, before replying: 'Yes, absolutely'.

I didn't just have Ian back, I had a motivated, committed and happy Ian back. He explained he was pleased to do whatever I wanted him to do for the business. I told him I wanted him to use his in-depth knowledge, mediation skills and expertise to bring on the next generation of family mediators within Mediate UK and he said he liked the sound of that.

Having Ian back on board, combined with Belinda's willingness to make the business work, completely transformed the company. I just needed to get myself sorted now.

I had already decided that the decision to hire a coach had been correct – I had just hired a terrible one. Right decision, wrong person. I also made a promise to myself that I would never put myself in such a risky situation as I had done at the

Travelodge. If I was ever in that dark place, I would get urgent help. Part of my new approach would be a commitment to change how I was. I would no longer hide my issues, but would discuss them openly. I would take complete control of my business and run it properly and professionally. I resolved to be the best manager I could be and to pull together a team of people who wanted to work for us and wanted us to be successful. I would use that awful experience in the Travelodge as a profound learning experience and I would keep it as a reminder of how I wanted to be a better person, better brother, better son, better dad and a far better boss. By now, I understood it wasn't anyone else's fault that the business was struggling, other than mine. It certainly wasn't Ian's fault, or Hannah's fault, or even Sean's. It was 100% my fault.

I needed to take full ownership and I would get the best help I could find to do that.

***

It was August 2019 and I was driving to Tring in Hampshire, with Amber.

'I'm worried they are going to ask me all sorts of questions about the business that I don't know the answer to,' she said.

'They won't,' I replied.

She was silent for a while and then spoke again. 'They won't ask me about VAT will they? I know fuck all about VAT.'

'They definitely won't be asking questions about VAT!' I reassured her.

Our first meeting with Simon Ellson, from ActionCOACH West Herts, lasted a little over two hours. During that time, we discussed the business, the recent experiences with Hannah and Sean and our plans and hopes for the future. We also explained how we were desperate to buy a property and how we needed to get the business to a place where we could save for a deposit and hopefully get a mortgage.

Simon explained how ActionCOACH works, the theory behind it and how it could help my business. This time, I had done my due diligence in full and Amber and I agreed to sign up.

Just three years later, Simon had helped Mediate UK achieve an increase in turnover of 800%. We have won four national business awards under his guidance. Luck finally played a part, as Simon is ranked as one of the top business coaches in the UK and is a multi-award winning coach himself.

I now had Simon helping me with important business decisions. I had Ian enthused and working his ass off to help the new mediators and improve all the company's processes, paperwork and IT. I had Belinda happily working away in a small office on her own, answering calls and emails, booking in clients and taking payments. In August 2019 we turned over twice as much as we had ever done in a single month and Belinda was still working away on her own without complaint. It was a breath of fresh air. In the October, when we tripled our previous best month, she admitted it may be a good idea to get some additional help in!

We hired a new member in the admin team and moved to a slightly bigger office. Business was continuing to grow and the new mediators were finding their feet. Simon was helping me to set up a proper business structure and systemise the whole business to allow it to scale. Ian was having a blast and doing what he enjoyed most. He would send me notes of encouragement, praise and thanks. I kept each and every one and they still mean the absolute world to me.

Belinda was getting better and more confident each day. As we celebrated the New Year in 2020, I was highly optimistic for the year ahead. Our new admin assistant had decided to leave, as she had issues at home with her family but we had recruited one of Belinda's friends, Jess, who was due to fly to the UK from South Africa and make a fresh start for herself. Jess had gone through our whole recruitment process and was easily the standout candidate. She would have breezed it, even if she had not been known to Belinda. Indeed, the fact they were friends put her at a disadvantage as I knew only too well some of the issues that can arise from hiring friends!

The news started mentioning an outbreak of something called Coronavirus in China but it didn't really impact us and was not something I was concerned about. As things developed in February, I looked at what would happen if we had a fully blown pandemic – and it wasn't great. But I figured if a mediation service goes under, then 70% of businesses would also go under that offered face-to-face contact with clients.

Meanwhile, Jess was travelling from South Africa via Dubai. With everything shutting down around her, she managed to hop on the last flight from Dubai to the UK and landed safely. By this time, Covid was a reality in the UK and Boris had held his national address locking down the country. Website hits and revenue fell by 80% in that two-week period. I needed to make the decision of whether I should actually still take on Jess at this time. I also knew that, if things continued as they were, we would only be able to survive for six months as a business.

Due to the upturn in the last six months of the previous year, and a good January, Amber and I had managed to put aside savings and we had some money for a deposit for the house I had promised her ten years earlier. Not much, but a start. I asked

Amber, 'if need be, shall we use that money to keep the business going and keep the staff on?' Amber didn't hesitate in her answer: 'Yes, absolutely.' The deal was done, then. We would take Jess on, albeit at reduced hours to those originally planned and she could help with marketing or other work for the business if she was not needed to cover the day-to-day office work. Turns out she *was* very much needed.

Meanwhile, I had to work out, once again, how to keep my business from going under.

'Nobody is gonna hit as hard as life, but it ain't how hard you can hit. It's how hard you can get hit and keep moving forward. It's how much you can take, and keep moving forward.'

— Rocky Balboa

13

THE COVID CRISIS

The last two weeks of March 2020 saw website hits, turnover and incoming phone calls decline by 80%. The country seemed to just freeze while people worked out what the fuck was going on. No one realistically expected the crisis to go on for over two years, however. I worked out we had enough to keep the staff on and pay our business expenses for six months. Then we would fold. I couldn't control what Covid was doing, or the Government, or anyone else for that matter. But I *could* control the decisions I made and my reaction to it. I wasn't prepared to have gone through all those years of pure shit, losing friends, losing my flats, losing money and almost losing my life, just to let it all go to pot because someone on the other side of the world ate a bat (allegedly).

I needed to use the few advantages I had. First of all, I was in control. I wasn't reliant on a boss or manager to tell me whether or not I could continue working or getting paid. That was a big factor – *I* was making the decisions.

Secondly, I found myself with time. And lots of it. We couldn't go out, couldn't see people, couldn't socialise … and I now had 80% less work than before. I had a gift that most people never get: time on my hands. I had the time to think and work **on** my business.

Finally, I had motivation in spades. I had six months to save the business, but also save our mediators from having no income and save our staff from becoming unemployed. I knew that any changes I needed to make would be embraced and welcomed by everyone at Mediate UK. I knew I would have everyone pulling together. I knew how powerful that could be in overcoming anything.

Be More Disney

Have you been to Disneyland? It's a great place, magical for kids and adults alike and we are very lucky that, at Disneyland Paris, our youngest Dexter gets an accessibility pass due to his autism – so we don't have to queue anywhere. And there are a lot of queues at Disneyland Paris!

However, the analogy I want to share is from a trip to Disneyland in Florida, where we spent a day when Dexter was just one year old. We had no autism diagnosis and no option of skipping the lines. As such, I had read a book that suggests, based on hours and hours of research, the best plan to 'do Disney' and tick off all the rides you want to experience without spending hours in tedious queues.

It involves arriving at the park early, then follow a set routine to get on all the rides you want to do. It tells you when to get fast passes, where to go first in the park and in what order. The plan worked a treat. For many of the most popular rides, we didn't even queue and then, when walking past them again, we saw there were queues of sixty minutes plus for exactly the same ride!

But the best tip was to leave the park about 1 pm, when it was getting really busy and extremely hot, and return to the villa for a swim, relaxing lunch and some chill-out time. I even took in a mid-afternoon power nap. Your parking ticket is valid for the whole day, so at 6pm we returned to the park. Walking against the crowds of sunburnt, tired, red-eyed families was fascinating. We were one of only about four families walking against the tide of exhausted people leaving Disneyland after a long day in the heat.

The evenings at the park are exciting, the lights are amazing and you have the laser and firework display at the end. I recommend, for any busy theme park, using the same strategy. It also now forms my analogy for business. If you find yourself walking against the crowd in any given situation, embrace it. Don't just follow everyone else. Be bold, be brave. Have a plan and follow it through, even if everyone else is doing something different. In most cases it will work and work well for you. Just like it did for our family at Disneyland that day.

I could see that many mediation companies were preparing to go into hibernation at the start of the Covid pandemic. The industry is made up of many small one or two-person businesses, with many mediators working part-time. Other companies were quite understandably reducing their overheads and costs and as so often happens, the first thing they cut was their marketing budget. Instead, Mediate UK decided to 'walk against the crowd'.

When lockdown started the weather was fantastic and as I sat down in the garden with a cold drink and my laptop, I wrote down on a piece of paper three things:

1. I won't let my business go under without a fight.
2. We are in a better position than many other businesses at this time.

3.   I'm going to go against the crowd.

I have found that writing things down in pen, in a notebook, helps to cement them in my mind and makes them easier to refer back to.

Before Covid, online mediation had been frowned upon by our governing body. It was considered not as good as meeting face-to-face and there were concerns about who else may be in the room; concerns children could overhear discussions and the ease with which people could just switch the meeting off if they got annoyed. It is far harder to walk out of a meeting room than to just click an off button. Especially for the client who stood up in one fraught mediation meeting, made a big speech about how he wished to never deal with his wife again and this was the final time she would ever lay eyes on him – before sheepishly returning to the meeting room to say the front door was locked and he couldn't work out how to get out of the building! I digress ...

We had been mediating online for a good five years and we had used Zoom before. We just needed to change all our processes and systems, train the mediators and promote the fact that we were still working, still available to mediate and help clients and, indeed, it was now even easier as online was the only option.

There was one small problem with the plan. The other mediation services that were not going into hibernation had also realised the opportunities. No longer were we competing against one or two local mediation services at our network of branches; suddenly every mediation service was competing against each other. The whole pool of England and Wales had opened up as potential areas to fish for new clients. The marketing we had done locally to attract clients just wouldn't work on a national level. We didn't have the funds for a Google ad campaign aimed at everyone in England and Wales. Indeed, we didn't have funds for *any* type of substantial marketing campaign.

Try Ranking on Google (No, that's not a typo!)

I figured that, with a lot of people sitting at home, a few things may happen.

1. We know that, when you are in an unhappy relationship, spending time with one another is usually a bad thing to do. It is one of the contributing factors as to why there is a peak for clients looking to get divorced in January and another, smaller, peak in September, after the summer holidays.

2. I knew if people were stuck at home, they would be using the internet more.

3. We had already attended a few online quizzes and people were getting more comfortable with using Zoom and other online software for meetings.

4. Parents would struggle with arrangements for children and may need help to sort out parenting plans.

I had a meeting with a marketing agency I had used before. Their owner, Tim, is one of the most respected gurus on marketing, especially digital marketing. Tim is the owner of Exposure Ninja, and they are well worth having a look at if you want to grow your business through digital marketing. Tim decided to speak with all their existing and recent clients at the start of lockdown and, by way of a throwaway comment at the end of the meeting, helped grow the visitors to my website by over 4000%!

'I can see online mediation is trending in searches at the moment. If I was you, I would be pushing that key phrase in a blog.'

Tim has been rather successful himself and, if someone of his calibre gives you a tip like that, you'd be stupid to turn it down. But I had written blogs before and not got any exposure for them. I always felt blog writing was like the amazing lemon cheesecake I made for the opening of the Scrummery. It looked fantastic, I was immensely proud of it and knew it had great contents, but no one, other than my own family, ever consumed it!

So I wrote the blog as Tim suggested. I then looked at how to promote a blog post. And that opened up my eyes to the complicated, bizarre and ultimately thrilling world of Search Engine Optimisation (SEO).

I could see from Google Analytics that our organic traffic – from people clicking on Google and other search engines – was pitiful. Most of our traffic was from paid advertising. I could also see that our organic traffic was extremely poor compared to most of our competitors.

If we were going to win the race for clicks, we needed to get ourselves to the top of Google for most of our key words as quickly as possible and certainly before the six months it would usually take for Google to recognise and rank new posts. We also needed to do it with no budget. This is the story of how we turned the Covid crisis into a benefit to not just save the business from going under, but to grow it and improve and change the lives of the people in it.

***

Two hundred? That's a lot, I thought to myself.

200 is the estimated number of factors that Google looks at when ranking a website. But we are going to break those 200 factors down into just three areas:

1. How good your site is overall (speed, look and whether it is mobile compatible).
2. The information that is on your site (blogs and content).
3. What other people think about your site (links and reviews).

A restaurant makes a great analogy here. Imagine you want some strawberries and cream.

1. You are far more likely to go to a restaurant in a good area, which looks nice from the outside and has many people already sitting in it. That's how good your website must be – you could serve the best strawberries and cream in the world, but if doing so from a shack in the back alley behind a kebab restaurant in a shitty part of town, you won't get as many clients.
2. The information on your site is the food in the restaurant. The strawberries and cream need to be fresh, delicious and geared towards people wanting strawberries and cream.
3. Imagine reading a review: *This restaurant is great. It serves the best strawberries and cream in the UK!* You are definitely going to that restaurant for your bowl of strawbs. (I need to confess that, while writing this analogy, I was eating a large bowl of strawberries and cream … and it was absolutely delicious.)

Google looks at your site in the same way. It will crawl it, evaluate it and then decide where you should be on the rankings for any key word you may want to have.

I decided that if I could hit as many of the 200 factors as possible, then Google would start to repay my work. During the Covid lockdowns, I added over 400,000 words of content to the website. I managed to get over 500 domains to link to my site, with over 1200 links. I increased my domain rating[1] from 9 in January 2020 to 26 in May 2022.

I had a contact who I knew could help with the technical side of SEO – what is called 'onsite SEO'. This involves meta tags, optimising page titles and making sure Google's web crawlers can find you and then navigate through your site easily.

My contact admitted that he had lost quite a few clients due to Covid as they had cut their budgets. *Brilliant*, I thought. We are going against the crowd. I knew then it was the right decision to make. He looked after all the technical stuff while I went off and tried to tick as many of the other factors as possible. I list these factors on the book's website www.greaterexpectations.life but the main thing I focused on was writing excellent content. Google wants to make the internet a better place for people using its search engine. This means if you write a fantastic piece of content, even if it is not keyword perfect, or doesn't have the 'right number of words', Google *will* ultimately reward you.

Using the tips that I have included in this book, I increased the number of our keywords that were number one on Google searches (called SERPS) from just 4 in April 2020 to 170 In April 2022. We have over 550 key words appearing on the first page of Google, up from 16 in the same period. This led to an increase in website visits of over 4000% and has been the key driver in allowing us to expand and invest in making our business the top-rated family mediation service in the UK – and now also the largest.

---

1 *Domain rating is a rather clumsy way of seeing how good your site is to Google. Each climb in number is harder, so it is a lot easier to get from 10 to 11 than from 20 to 21. But it's a good indication of where you are. As a guide, YouTube is currently 100, LinkedIn is 99 and, rather brilliantly, Pornhub is 69.*

Thank goodness those pills didn't have the intended effect in that Travelodge.

Some people have commented that the increase in business must have been down to Covid and the number of people arguing over children and subsequently getting divorced. This was not the case. The number of divorces in the UK did not increase following the Covid lockdowns. And we actually dealt with very few cases regarding child arrangements due to the Covid restrictions. The key changes were: the ability to offer an online service; the fact people felt more comfortable holding important meetings online; and the time it gave me to focus *on* the business and build up the content while working on the other SEO factors.

I challenged myself to improve just one piece of the business each week. Some of these improvements would be substantial, like taking on a new member of the team or an office move, but others more subtle – like changing the wording on an email template, or making a process clearer to explain to clients.

I figured that if I made just one positive change to the business each week, after a year we would have improved over fifty areas. In reality, one change leads to another and in many cases, the changes are cumulative, so the improvements multiply and compound. Our business looks nothing like it did just three months ago and will look different again in another three months. That takes a commitment to constant change and innovation and a team who are willing to embrace change with the flexibility and desire to help you carry out those changes and implement them correctly.

In 2020, we grew the admin team from one member of staff in the February to three, when Danielle - Belinda's youngest sister – joined us shortly after Jess. Danielle is fantastic at any admin tasks and her sense of humour, spirit and love for life lifted the whole team. She is also a believer in goal setting and achieving more in life, has a psychology degree and a great business brain. The potential in Danielle is ridiculous and, while she hasn't recognised it herself yet, she is one of the most amazing young people I have met. It's one of the key reasons I poached her for my new company, YAKKA (which I'll talk about more in later chapters). She subsequently became a co-founder of YAKKA and one of my best friends.

By 2022, we had seven people working in the head office to help our clients and sixteen family mediators. We had also expanded to forty branches nationally. During this period, I was able to give Belinda a 40% pay rise and promote her to Business Support Manager. In October 2022, I promoted her again to be Managing Director of Mediate UK. All of this took place within three-and-a-half years and all from being offered a position as a job-share admin assistant!

The promotions helped in a small way contribute towards Belinda getting a mortgage and buying her own home, the very goal she had told us about when she first joined Mediate UK. I couldn't have been happier for her and her family when she completed on that house. One of the things I am most proud of was being able to afford to buy private health insurance for the team. I got a moving email from Danielle when she had a health scare and was able to get it seen to immediately due to the private insurance cover in place. Those moments stay with me and make me feel that it was worth all those years of struggle.

Ian still sends me notes, emails and gifts, telling me how much he is enjoying his work. My favourite moment in the past ten years was being able to give Ian a pay rise and one day off each week to help him focus on his family and I love being able to give him a good bonus each Christmas. He deserves every penny and moment of acknowledgement as he has been absolutely critical to the success of Mediate UK. Simply put, I couldn't have done any of this without him. I feel honoured to call him a friend.

Then back to Jess. The decision to employ her, even at a time when no one else was recruiting and we had just suffered a drop in business of 80%, was without a doubt one of the best hiring decisions I have made (I can't take the credit for hiring Belinda, as Sean the fraudster business coach hired her). Jess has gone on to be not only an excellent member of the business support team, she is now working part of the week as Director of Marketing. Her knowledge of the business is amazing. Her commitment to our clients is fantastic and her sense of humour brings the best out of the whole team. I am in the lucky position of having excellent people now running the business – and running it better than I ever managed to. It really is all about getting the right people in the right environment with the right motivation... and amazing things will happen.

All the team's dedication to their work just drives me on to work harder, better and smarter so that we have the best possible business for them to work in and with the best possible benefits that we can afford.

This year, on handing out our Christmas bonuses, I got a message from Danielle, when I told her that I hoped YAKKA would be a success and change all our lives:

> ... you already changed our lives. You gave Belinda the opportunity to believe in herself and reach her true potential, and she is now Managing Director. Something she never would have thought capable or fitting to her. You set Jess up in a new country, and gave her a family. You've pushed/are stilling pushing me out of my comfort zone and making me

take on new challenges head on which is bettering both my personal and professional life each day. You also gave us all a friend, and changed the game on how bosses SHOULD treat their employees. You deserve the success of YAKKA, and if that brings us success too, then BONUS."

I sat at my laptop and cried when I received the message. Just like I had done so many times over ten years of struggle. But this time was different. They were tears of happiness.

You see, it had just dawned on me that, as it turns out, I didn't need to achieve a higher turnover milestone, open a set number of branches, reach a better net profit margin or even have a fixed sum of money in the bank account to be happy. Yes, they are all important measures of how well your business is performing. But my barometer to measure success had been wrong all those years. The goal I had achieved was better than all of those metrics. I'd managed to pull together an amazing team of people and they genuinely appreciated that. I finally felt I had achieved something in my business life. There was a purpose to my existence after all. For the first time in my life, I felt worthwhile.

I see a distinct irony that my previous memory of South Africa was getting inappropriately fiddled with by a fat fingered pervert, in a position of trust before being sent home in disgrace. My memory of South Africa is quite different now.

It's about how three people, originally from that country, delivered so much energy, passion and commitment into my business, they not only saved it from failing but, by doing so, they – along with my amazing friend Ian – saved me too. Wow.

'The more you know who you are, and what you want, the less you let things upset you.'

— Bob Harris, *Lost in Translation*

PART THREE
WHAT YOU NOW NEED TO DO

14

SETTING YOUR OWN 'GREATER EXPECTATIONS'

Goal Setting

If I can give you just one piece of advice, one action point to take away from reading this book, it is to undertake the following goal setting task. You can visit www.greaterexpectations.life to download the PDF for free. I am pushing this one area, not because I will make anything from it, but because this is the one thing you can do that will make the biggest change to your life and potentially the life of your family and others in the world.

By working out and recording your goals you will be in the tiniest minority of people. Less than 3% of the population write and record their goals, let alone commit and take action to achieve them. I talked before about the advantage of going against the crowd. This is one area where you can easily achieve that and go against the 97% of humans that don't do what you are hopefully about to do.

Harvard Business School carried out a study of students in 1979. It is often quoted in business and personal development books, but I repeat it here in case you have not come across it. The study showed that prior to graduation:

- 84% of the entire class had set no goals at all
- 13% of the class had set written goals but had no concrete plans to achieve them
- 3% of the class had both written goals and concrete plans and action points to achieve them

Ten years later and the same class were analysed on their income. The 13% of students who had written goals were making twice as much money as the 84% who did not have any set goals at all. But here is the highlight: the 3% who had set goals and had a plan to achieve them were taking home **an average of 10x the income of the rest of the class together.** Please – write down your goals and do this exercise. For you and for your family.

Other advantages of goal setting

Doing this goal setting exercise with your partner, even if you have been with them for many years, can do amazing things for your relationship. It can throw up all sorts of conversations. 'I never realised you wanted to go to Santorini, me too!' You can also celebrate each other's goals and achievements as you start to tick them off – and you *will* tick them off, believe me. I never thought I would hear myself congratulate my wife on buying a horse trailer, but I knew it was one of her top fifty goals in life, one that was important to her and one that she was desperate to achieve. How much better is that knowledge, rather than my previous response, which would have been: 'A trailer? How much did that cost?!'

It's an even better exercise to do with someone you have recently met, or are considering committing to. OK, probably not a great idea to whip out the PDF at your first date, over dinner – 'I need you to write down your top fifty goals, before I will even consider ordering dessert' – but you don't want to be settling down with someone who has completely different aims in life, especially if your main goal is to visit every continent on earth and theirs is to finish the full box set of *Married at First Sight, UK.* Having your own goals is great. Having aligned goals with someone you are spending your time and possibly your whole life, with is amazingly powerful. Please, do it.

How to set goals

If you have worked for any large corporation, you will probably have heard of the acronym SMART. It stands for Specific, Measurable, Achievable, Relevant and Timely. In one of my jobs, they changed the acronym to SMAART and then again to SMAAART. I have absolutely no idea what the extra A's stood for and I don't think the managers did either.

To me, SMART goals just remind me of working for shit companies, or having pointless 1-2-1 meetings with a manager so they can tick a box for human resources and revisit it again in twelve months. They were mostly forgotten about as soon as they were written down. But there was some sound theory behind the acronym. I am going to ask you to look at the following examples and apply them to your own goals when you do this exercise (we have already agreed you are going to do this, right?)

Specific:

NO: I want to lose weight

YES: I want to lose seven pounds in two months

Measurable:

NO: I want to be financially secure

YES: I want to have a net worth of £22 million

Achievable:

> NO: I want to have world peace

> YES: I want to be kind to everyone I meet, even if they are not kind to me

Relevant:

> NO: I'm going to read one Katie Price penned novel per month for a whole year

> YES: I'm going to read one self-help or business book per month for a whole year

Timely:

> NO: I'm going to write my own book

> YES: I'm going to write a book and complete the initial draft by October 2022 and have it ready for publishing by December 2023.

I may have been a bit harsh on Katie Price in those examples. If that really is your goal, we are not judging. Honest.

Setting your greater expectations

These are the first three steps in achieving your goals and leading a better life.

Step One – Download the goal-setting PDF from www.greaterexpectations.life

Step Two – Complete the exercise, preferably with your partner

Step Three – Start ticking the goals off, one by one

Let's look at this in a little more detail. I firstly need to confess that this exercise is not completely my own work. It has been adapted and expanded from the goal setting exercise suggested by Jim Rohn. If you haven't heard of Jim Rohn, he was an American entrepreneur, author and speaker who is credited with helping thousands of people with their personal development: not least Mark R. Hughes, the creator of Herbalife, and Tony Robbins. If you haven't heard of Tony Robbins, there is a chapter dedicated to him in this book as well.

I have adapted and developed Jim Rohn's suggestions, to what I consider to be the best process for me. It worked, so I want you to try it as well with the same confidence that I do. For the sake of the walk-through below, I am going to presume you are doing this with your partner, but you don't have to. If you are single and want to have a partner in your life, well, imagine how your stake will rise once you have started ticking off some of these goals.

The following exercise is best done with a glass of something you enjoy, a pen and paper each (old fashioned, I know, but a laptop creates a barrier between you and phones just don't work as well) and you can do it as part of a date night after a nice meal, perhaps. You will need at least two hours. It should be fun and something you work on together.

You are going to start by writing down five things you have already accomplished that you are proud of. This may be something you have learnt, something you have overcome, something you have birthed or cared for, or a relationship you are proud to have with someone.

Well done – that wasn't that hard was it? Now read these out to each other and try not to get into an argument if one of you wrote down I'm proud of my relationship with my spouse, and the other just listed they were proud of getting their golf handicap down to single digits.

Next up is the goal setting part. You are going to need fifty in total here. Why fifty? Well part of the point of the exercise is to get your brain thinking. Anyone can think of five or ten goals. Fifty is going to take a bit of brain power, deeper thinking and soul searching. It also allows you to include some goals that you can achieve relatively easily. One of my goals was to drink a bottle of wine priced over £50 from a supermarket and have it with a nice fillet steak. Two weeks later, I was drinking the wine (£50 reduced to £35 at Waitrose, still counts and win-win) and enjoying the steak with a peppercorn sauce and my in-laws. (I wasn't eating my in-laws; they were invited as Amber doesn't like red wine and I didn't want to guzzle the 2004 Chateau Tour-Robert all by myself).

When completing the goals, remember the SMART analogy. 'I want to play rugby for England' is probably not achievable, unless you are young and very good at rugby. But 'I want to have a box at Twickenham to watch the rugby', or 'go on an organised trip with the next British Lions Rugby tour' *is* achievable.

You will get to a point, maybe about twenty goals in, where you are struggling. This is a good time to cheat and plagiarise each other's goals. Yes, copying is allowed and positively encouraged in this exercise. If you are in any way similar souls, that should get you an extra five or so goals to add and you are approximately halfway there already.

You will get to a stage where you think about travel and I encourage you to add some places you want to visit, both near and far, expensive and less so. But this is not purely a travel exercise and, while you may be tempted to fill up your fifty with places you would like to visit, I encourage you to limit this to a maximum of ten travel-orientated goals.

Your goals don't all need to be about you, you selfish princess! They can be about helping others. 'I want to commit 10% of my income to charitable causes.' 'I want to support my son or daughter to pass their GCSEs' or 'I want to support them getting into Nottingham University to study Applied Physics'. All of those are good examples of goals you may wish to include that help others.

You will probably dry up about forty goals in. That's fine and normal. You should definitely swap notes again at this stage and discuss what you have written down between you. Spend some more time on your final few goals and don't forget to include some relatively easy ones to achieve. 'I want to call my mum each week', or 'I want to eat at that new Italian restaurant in town' are fine. The reason for this is that your brain will continue working on the exercise and you will wake up in the middle of the night, announcing: 'The boat, I forgot to mention I want to buy a yacht and moor it in Portofino!' You can then return to your list and scribble out one of the hastily added goals (i.e. 'call my mum each week') and replace it with the luxury yacht. Oh, and – sorry mum – but it will have four cabins and a great berth location.

You should now have your fifty goals. Well done – you are already in the top 13% of people who write their goals down. We now need to allocate a time scale to them and score them on how important they are.

Timescales

To make this easier for you we are going to give you some options. Simply enter that you will achieve the goal within one year, three years, five years or more – or for anything else put ten.

Importance

Use the following table to then list how important each goal is to achieve.

1	It would be nice to achieve this goal
2	I would feel good if I achieved this goal
3	I would feel happy if I achieved this goal
4	This goal would make me feel proud of myself
5	This goal would make me feel proud and potentially help others
6	This goal would bring genuine joy to me and/or others
7	This goal would make me feel I had achieved something special in my life
8	Achieving this goal would make a genuine difference to my or other's life
9	Achieving this goal is massively important to me and would completely change my life
10	I absolutely *must* achieve this goal. I will not feel I have achieved in life if I don't. It would make a life-changing difference to my and other's lives

You should now have a list of goals with a timescale attached to them and a score reflecting how important they are. By now you may be on your second bottle of Prosecco, but bear with me, the important stuff is about to come.

Counting

I want you to count up how many goals you have for each timescale: one, three, five or ten years. You may end up with a box like this:

	1 Year	3 Year	5 Year +	10 Year +
No. of Goals	12	15	16	7

This allows you to see how many goals you need to achieve within the next year and your goals should be spread out over this time. If you have forty-eight in year one, or forty-five in year ten plus, then you are either giving yourself a bit of a sudden challenge or delaying your achievement for a little too long.

Revisit your plan if you need to at this stage, and if you do have the same goals as your partner, it probably makes sense to allocate the same timescales to them. Unless you really want to travel to Santorini in separate years, of course!

Your Reason

The final task is the most important step. I appreciate you may be tired and a little drunk – and if one of your joint goals is to 'inject more passion into our relationship', with priority 9 within the next ten minutes, you will be keen to start ticking off some of the goals already. But this final stage is absolutely key to you achieving your goals. As, let's face it, you don't want to have just a bucket list. You want to have a plan.

We are going to do this step in two parts, choosing two goals from your year one list and two other goals from the remainder. So, for four goals in total, I want you to write down the following:

Goal 1

Why is this goal important to you?

What is this goal for? What purpose will it serve? Who will benefit?

What must I do or become to achieve this goal? What action or steps must I take now?

To reiterate. You are going to do this for the top-two-scored goals for your year one and then your top-two-scored goals for the remaining years. These goals are likely to be scored 8+ so you don't have to start thinking about why eating at the new

Italian is going to benefit your family, or what steps you need to take to secure a reservation there!

If you can commit to your brain that this goal needs to be achieved and, in doing so, will benefit others, you are far more likely to achieve it. I'll give an example of one of my answers:

Goal 1 – Grow YAKKA to 1 million users worldwide by April 2025.

Why is this goal important to you?

It's a milestone that will mean YAKKA has been adopted and liked by the users. It will give us something to take to investors or possible purchasers of the app. It will show that my idea for YAKKA has been a success.

What is this goal for? What purpose will it serve? Who will benefit?

I believe having one million people connected throughout the world; meeting up in person either for a 1-2-1 get together, an activity or a group event, will make the world better. A million users will mean we have a great business and I can start to take an income from it, helping my family and friends. I will be able to buy that house I promised my wife all those years ago. It will benefit Simon, Danielle and anyone on the team and repay them for their faith and hard work in building YAKKA. It will make me feel worthwhile and successful.

What must I do or become to achieve this goal? What action or steps must I take now?

I need to keep redeveloping YAKKA until we have an MVP. I need to continue to listen to our users' feedback and make something they want to use. I need to keep raising my vision and seeing the end result, without getting tied down in the detail. I need to grow a fantastic team around me and support and nurture them so we are all working toward the same result of 1 million users. I need to make sure I am the best I can be for the journey and focus on my health, building my knowledge and keep showing up every day.

You need to do this more in-depth analysis of your top-two one year goals and your top-two other timescale goals. Yes, it's extra work. Yes, it's 100% worth the effort. It will get your brain set up to start making the goals a reality.

Push, don't pull

The way you word your goals is also important. Your mindset will shift significantly if you say; 'I will become healthy and only put things in my body that benefit it', rather than 'I hope to *give up* smoking.' Or, I will have a net worth of £22 million, rather than 'I never want to be poor again.' Keep your goals positive and definite when writing them. It can make all the difference to how your brain helps you achieve them.

The flip side of the coin

There is usually a flip side to everything in life. Enjoyed a lovely night out on the town? Don't enjoy the hangover the next morning. Enjoy racing after criminals on blues and twos? Don't enjoy the paperwork that follows. Enjoy writing down your list of life goals and picturing how amazing you will make your life? Don't enjoy thinking about where you currently are in life.

Creating, discussing and writing down your goals will make them far more achievable than not doing anything. It can also be a slap in the face to remind you of how far away you are from achieving them. To avoid beating up on yourself because you are miles away from purchasing the villa in Italy; the Aston Martin or the Rolex watch, it is important you also put goals down that can be achieved relatively quickly and easily. Buying (and reading) that book, eating at that cool restaurant or calling that friend you haven't spoken to in a long time are all good examples of goals that could be important to your progress but don't require a multi-million pound exit from a start-up to achieve.

Ticking off some of your goals early will give your brain a dopamine hit and push it to work out ways to tick more goals off. You can also break your larger goals down into more manageable ones. Writing a novel is a large goal to achieve. Writing the first chapter is a far more achievable goal and more likely to get done.

What happens next?

Do you just file the list of goals away in a drawer, perhaps? Stick it on the wall? Post it on Instagram?

Well, the first thing is you will most likely have missed out a few obvious ones and will need to re-do some goals within the next day or so. That's fine, no one is marking this for you. But once you have your list and your four goals for which you have earmarked the reason why you are doing them and what you need to do, you need to take at least one action for each of these most important goals.

It may be to buy a book on marketing. Or sign up for a course. Buy a website domain name for the business you intend to launch. Make a phone call to someone. Do whatever action point you need to take to move you one step closer towards that goal. That is just four action points in total and you need to do this within forty-eight hours of finishing your goal list. Yes, I assure you anyone can take just four small steps in a single forty-eight-hour period to make their most important life goals come true. If you don't have time, you need to get up thirty minutes earlier, go to bed thirty minutes later, miss a TV programme or even have lunch at your desk.

It is imperative that you take that first step towards achieving these most important goals while your brain is busy trying to work out a way to achieve them.

Your brain

It's a pretty amazing thing. I was unlucky enough to witness an autopsy when I started in the police. The pathologist absent-mindedly cut open the back of the skull, and rolling the face forward like a latex mask, proceeded to pull out the brain from the back of the head. I should point out that the poor chap was dead, having succumbed to throat cancer on a flight from the US to London Heathrow.

Chatting away to us, the pathologist then held the brain in his left hand, while slicing it open with a super-sharp knife in his right hand. The brain looks like a highly whisked and set blancmange, grey in colour, soft and full of fat. It is the fattiest organ in your body, weighing in at three pounds and it is 75% water. The pathologist simply sliced it up, checked everything was OK with a quick glance and then shoved it into a small green bag with the other internal organs of our deceased subject.

The brain itself contains over 80 billion neurons. Their job is to make connections with other neurons, which over time could make up to 1,000 trillion connections. When a neuron is stimulated, it transmits data at an impressive 268 miles per hour. I never even reached half that speed when driving in the police. Honest.

Because you have created a list of things to do, your brain is automatically trying to work out a way so that you can tick all fifty goals to show you have achieved them. Why? Because your brain knows a list is something that has to be acted on and is already starting to pre-empt it for you. Yes, even while you are sleeping, your brain is working out ways to achieve your goals. And all because you wrote them down and placed importance against them.

You may have heard of the placebo effect? It is a proven scientific fact that placebos work and some doctors even prescribe placebo medication for some illnesses, especially around IBS, depression and anxiety. But let's look at an example involving erections. (Don't worry, it's not hard). Ahem.

In one published study, male participants who were suffering with erectile dysfunction were split into three groups. The first group was told they would receive a treatment for erectile dysfunction. The second group were told they would receive either a placebo or an actual pill to help them achieve an erection, and the third group was told they would just receive a placebo.

All three groups were, in fact, given starch tablets, with no associated benefit to achieving or maintaining an erection. (I love that phrase achieving an erection, I doubt many of you listed that in your top five achievements to date, but if you did – good on you. Keep it up!)

The outcome from the experiment was that the level of erectile dysfunction in *all three groups* improved. Yes, placebos work so well that even the group who knew it was a placebo saw positive results. It was a really uplifting experience for them all … I'll stop now.

So if we accept, as scientists do, that our brains can cure a symptom just by believing a pill that has nothing to do with the ailment can cure it – even when we know that it is just a placebo, imagine what your brain can do when told that the goals you have listed are achievable within a certain timeframe and have a priority of 9 or 10 to achieve. I assure you; it will start working on solving that problem while you are still clearing away the dishes from your dinner.

Here's another thing. If you start putting your intentions out into the universe, speaking them to others (another reason why the exercise is best done with a partner, even if you are not romantically involved) and writing them down, you start a process of making them more achievable, and when you put things out there, the universe has a habit of responding. I promise you it works and that is about as spiritual as you will get from me.

Some of you reading this book may be religious, but you may recall from Chapter One, that I am not. The process I describe is called 'manifesting' and it is, without a doubt, 'a thing'. I assure you. If a starch pill can cure your IBS, by making your brain think it is curing your IBS and therefore your IBS is cured by your body, *even when you know it is only a starch pill* … surely the same can be true of manifesting your goals? You want the desired outcome to be so clear, so natural and so assured in its eventual outcome, that when it does happen it comes as no surprise whatsoever.

Professional athletes do this all the time, envisioning the perfect served ace, clearing the high jump bar or scoring the penalty. Call it 'visioning', call it 'manifesting' or call it the 'law of attraction'. When you tell the world you want something badly enough, the world will help conspire to get it for you. If you download the goal setting exercise from www. greaterexpectations.life, it includes a section on manifesting your top goal. I hope you give it a go.

I didn't understand any of this, when I did my first goal setting example some fifteen years ago. I was separated from my first wife, had decided I wanted to leave the police and set up my own business and had read about the importance of goal setting. The book I had read suggested making a vision board of all the stuff you wanted to achieve or get in life.

Being new to this, and also very shallow at that time, I carefully printed, cut out and stuck to a white A3 card an Aston Martin DB7, a superyacht, a luxury mansion, a wad of cash, and a blonde-haired model in a bikini with ample frontage. I threw in some other pictures of designer clothes, watches etc. – just to make sure all the board was covered – and I pinned it to my notice board above my computer desk.

You can only imagine my disappointment when I woke up the next day and I had not received one single item from my vision board! *What a load of nonsense*, I thought. A week later I threw it away in the bin. Load of mumbo jumbo.

But, as we know, the Christmas that followed shortly after that doomed experiment was one of the worst I had experienced, and the New Year's Eve party I attended I left early feeling down, lonely and depressed. As the clock struck midnight, I was in bed thinking about what actions I could take to make my life better. I wanted a partner and knew I was unlikely to find one in the police or at a pub. The next morning, I set myself up a profile on match.com and promised myself I would go on as many dates as it would take to find the right person for me, and I hoped they would feel the same. Let's take a look at the process:

I took action – I wrote down, or in this case, printed and cut out the image of what I was looking for.

I took a step to achieve it – I signed up for an online dating service and started going on dates.

I manifested – I envisaged what my date would look like, what we would say, eat and drink and how we would be happy and love one another.

Less than six weeks later, I knocked on the door of Amber's house and the rest is history. At the time Amber had dark hair, but she had been a successful model before we met, with long blonde hair, and looked scarily similar to the girl in that photo I had printed. I focused on what I wanted, I put it out to the universe, I manifested the image and I found the love of my life.

There is only one thing stopping you from achieving those goals that are the most important to you. And that one thing is … you. Get absolute certainty that it will happen, imagine exactly what it looks like when it does happen and your brain and the universe will conspire to make it happen. Go to www. greaterexpectations.life to see my goals and how I managed to tick some of them off.

Revise and Revisit

You need to update this exercise every three-to-four months. You can, of course, tick things off as you achieve the goal, or you can wait to do more in one go at your next visit. But the one thing you cannot do is put the goal list away and forget about it.

You may find that some of the goals that were really important to you have become less so. You may have new goals or plans that you need to include. And – best of all – you may have ticked some off. If you have an out-of-date goal that is no longer relevant, replace it with a new, more relevant goal and remember to score the importance and allocate a time slot to achieve it within. Celebrate each goal you have been able to tick off. You can leave them on there, showing them as achieved. You want to look back at this list in five or ten years' time and see how far you have come, what you have achieved and how writing down, visioning and taking action to achieve your dreams really does work. Just like a pill made of starch can give you a super-strong erection if you believe it will. Give it a go and see what happens (the goal setting that is, the starch-pill option is purely up to you).

'Setting goals is the first step in turning the invisible into the visible.'

— Tony Robbins

15

STARTING YOUR OWN BUSINESS

The three biggest obstacles to starting a business, for most people, are – in no particular order:

1. I don't have the time
2. I don't have the money
3. I don't have the idea

We'll look at these individually, but first of all let us assume you have got all your pillars of support in place. You now need to figuratively lay yourself on top of this support and build your business up from you. The diagram below makes it easier to envisage:

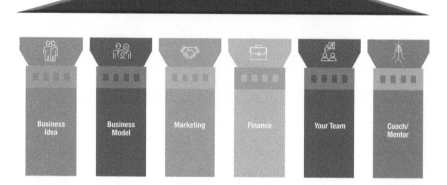

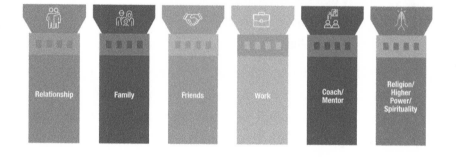

Your business is going to consist of the following six pillars:

- Your business idea – what it is you are actually going to do or sell

- Your business model – how you are going to sell it

- Your marketing – how you are going to let people know about it

- Your finances – how you will fund your plan and make money from your business

- Your team – how you will find and train the people to make it work
- Your coach or mentor – who you are going to use for help, guidance and advice

And all of these need to be put into a business plan. You may remember Hannibal from the A-Team's catchphrase was 'I love it when a plan comes together.' Well, so do business owners, investors and shareholders. You need to have a plan of what you are going to do – even if you are setting up a small cleaning service. You will find that, with a plan, you will work less, execute better and stay focused. There are loads of plans you can download from the internet. I'll be honest – most of them are a bit boring to complete and it is difficult to find a 'one size fits all' template. And, let's be honest, while forecasting is important, if you haven't even got your business up and running yet, estimating what your turnover and profit will be after five years is complete and utter guesswork.

We have devised a very simple and easy-to-complete one page business plan template at www.greaterexpectations.life and it is free to download. Feel free to download and start recording your thoughts on paper.

In the next few chapters I am going to take you through the objections to starting a business, the six pillars of the business you need to get right and how to build a business plan. But before we do any of that, I want to look at whether or not you should even start a business of your own, and if so, what type of business should you aim for?

Should I really start my own business?

I am going to make an assumption that in your goal setting exercise, which you completed in the last chapter (you did complete that, right?), that there is at least one goal that will require a lot of money. Probably more than you could pay from your existing savings. Am I right? Even, and I really am not listening to your excuses right now, if you haven't done the exercise yet, you can probably think of something right now that you would like to do, or have, or gift, that would require a lot of money that you do not currently have.

So how do you achieve those goals? Credit card perhaps – the antithesis of money management (unless you are buying a two-bedroom maisonette with five of them, as I decided to do in 2008, oops)!

No, you will need to earn a lot of money from your job or from running your own business. Let's look at my previous job in the Met Police and one of my goals. To own a five-bedroom house for my family near where I currently live. For that, I would need £600,000. And I have a 10% deposit, so I need a mortgage of £540,000.

I have managed to find a mortgage company willing to offer me up to 4.5 times my salary. So I need to earn £120,000 per year. The trouble is, I am a police officer, and I earn only £31,000, having just completed my two-year probation. No problem, I put it under a five-year plan, so I have plenty of time to work hard and get promoted.

Let's take a look at what I would need to do. To earn anywhere near that amount, I would need to be what they call an ACPO rank officer. This rank is from Commander up to the Commissioner. The trouble is, there are only 34 of these positions in the Met. As of 2018 there were 30,390 police officers of all rank in the Met police. That means you have about a one in 894 chance of becoming an ACPO rank and earning enough to have a chance at getting a five-bedroom house valued at £600,000. (I appreciate anyone within a reasonable commute of London would say you cannot get anywhere near a five-bedroom house for £600,000, but in my imaginary example I travel each week from Rugby, only a thirty-minute trip into London Euston, and I stay with family when working shifts, so, neh!)

I would suggest that those odds are not particularly in your favour. You would also need to completely give up your life for 'the job' (that's what police officers call the job of being a police officer – 'the job', we're an intelligent lot). You would also need to network, be extremely lucky, highly intelligent, a world-class leader and, in fact, every skillset you would need to become a successful entrepreneur!

The difference here is: to achieve that goal, you are up against 30,000 other police officers all vying and hoping to get promoted (and to get that level it would take a long time of service, usually twenty years plus), in order to even have a stab at achieving your goal.

Or you can quit the police and set up your own business. Just do it a lot better than I did originally and ensure you read this book first and carry out the instructions to the letter. Please.

If you are lucky enough to get paid for a job that you absolutely love and you are happy in your life and with what you have, then you are the richest person in the world. I genuinely mean that. You have got it well and truly cracked. You have a job you enjoy and look forward to, you may be performing a role that serves a higher purpose, such as nurse, teacher or scientist. You get paid each month on the dot. You get a pension, paid holidays, and a certainty in your life that can provide you peace and comfort. You are the lucky ones. While I encountered many of these people in the Met, I know that they are few and far between and they are extremely unlikely to be reading this book.

No, the majority of people are stuck in job that they hate, that they want to progress in but cannot. A job that does not pay them enough to meet their reasonable needs, let alone pay for any goals in their life. So they crack on, in the hope that one day they will win the EuroMillions lottery (hey it could be you, but trust me, it won't be, not at odds of 140,000,000 to 1).

Many people set up their own business and are happy working for themselves. Again, if this is you, and it makes you happy, then that is amazing. Most people who work for themselves, though, have a total asshole for a boss! You want to go on holiday, you don't get paid. So you need to find cover, but they can't do it as well as you. Plus you have to do tax returns, deal with marketing, accountants, complaints, stupid customers. No, it's all too much. For many, the dream of being self-employed just means you have less security and more aggravation.

Another option is to franchise. Done properly, with the right franchise, this can work really well. Examples of great franchises in the UK are McDonald's, Toni & Guy, ActionCOACH and Clarks Shoes. All offer you the chance to work for yourself, but using their proven marketing, processes, structure and training. Of course, this comes with a fee. The average amount required to set up a McDonald's is £750,000 and, if you had that amount of money or could borrow it, well.... You would already be able to purchase your own five-bedroom house as per your goals.

Most franchises require you to pay a commission each month to the parent company and they have strict rules within which you need to operate. A franchise can be a great option for you, especially if you have the money upfront. It is usually a safer option. Most entrepreneurs I have met want to have the flexibility to operate within their own rules and keep 100% of the money they make. Wouldn't you rather be the one selling your proven business model as a franchise to a franchisee?

Another option, popular today, is to be an expert or celebrity. This category would include professional footballers, actors, influencers, YouTube hosts, reality TV stars, even some business coaches and anyone who builds a brand around themselves. You will normally need to be an expert in your field or have a talent that other people want to buy or consume.

Entrepreneur

This is the category where I put myself and where I reckon you stand the best chance of achieving your goals, if your goals include anything expensive. Simply put, it's your best shot at achieving the life you want.

The levels of life

Take a look at the graphic on this page. Which level do you currently fall into?

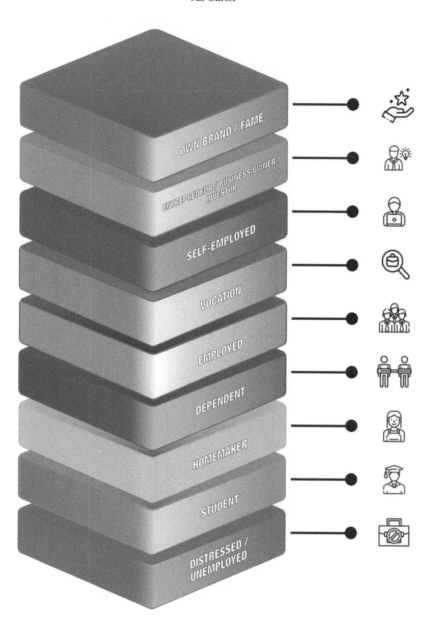

Which level would you *like* to be on?

Greater Expectations

There is no right or wrong answer, of course. For most people, the level you are currently on is a choice you have made. In exactly the same way, where you *want* to be is a choice you can – and should – be making. It is quite possible that you can fall into one or more categories.

Some students will be in the 'dependent' category, but may have a part-time job in a bar at the weekend. They would fall into two categories. At the top end, David Beckham is an expert, having mastered his trade, has a very successful own-brand and fame and is also an investor, entrepreneur and business owner. He falls into all three of the top levels.

Let's look at each level in a bit more detail:

Distressed / Unemployed:

Distressed people are those who have dropped out of society. The street drinker, the drug addict, the homeless or the criminal. I came across many of these people during my time in the police. I remember being shocked at a street drinker who I could have sworn was sixty-five and who gave his age in the custody suite as thirty-nine. He had a room at a local hostel but was only allowed to stay there if he was not drinking. He was so dependent on alcohol, he chose to sleep rough by the river Thames, rather than take up the option of a more comfortable bed. If you are in this category, you are probably not reading this book.

If you are unemployed then I hope you *are* reading this book and that it provides you with some hope and inspiration for your successful future.

Students:

This covers those at university or those studying to further their knowledge. They will usually pay for their studies, in the hope

223

that it will further their chosen career path. Indeed, for many, they will have to have completed this section in order to even be considered for their chosen career, such as electrician, police officer, teacher or doctor.

Homemaker:

These are the people who stay at home to raise children and look after the family home. It has conventionally fallen to women, but not always and in recent years, excitingly, less so. It is an often underrated role in society − even frowned upon by some. This is the role Amber took in our lives and was vital to make sure our children were happy and healthy, especially Dexter with his diagnosis of autism. It also crucially provided the foundation and support I needed to help build my businesses.

Dependent:

This category covers anyone under the age of sixteen who would not be able to fend for themselves in society yet, as they are too young to get a full-time job. It also covers those who, through disability, mental health, or other issues, are unable to work. This category needs help and support from family, society and the government to survive. This category is important as it is where the proceeds from the other categories should be directed. We should always look to help those less fortunate than ourselves, who act as a reminder of how fortunate we are in life, even if we don't appreciate that all the time in our own heads.

Employed:

This is the largest and most popular category. In June 2022, 29.6 million people in the UK fell into this category − 76% of the population. It's the category that our education system is geared up towards putting you in. Having a safe, secure job is seen as a positive thing. Your family will be pleased for you. Proud parents will talk about you. It provides security for you and your family. You get paid even if you are sick or when you go on holiday. What's not to love?

But there is a downside to being in this category: you will always be sacrificing time for money. You might not actually be paid a certain amount per hour, but you are still giving up your life to receive a wage that is less than the total output you are generating. Why else would someone be paying you otherwise?

Oh and, of course, you may be made redundant, fired or let go, the business may collapse or be taken over or you might be furloughed at 80% pay – and those decisions are completely out of your control. You are, in effect, 100% reliant on someone else to provide for you and your family.

Vocation:

This category is what I call 'the nirvana'. The nirvana group are people who are doing something they absolutely love and getting paid for it. This could be anything – it is, after all, down to the individual to decide what makes them happy in life. But popular choices would be the sportsperson – not quite renowned enough for the fame section, but doing a sport they love and getting paid. It could be the police officer, nurse, vet, charity worker, armed forces or anyone who does a job that they adore doing.

Indeed, they would continue doing the job even if they won the lottery. And this was exactly how I felt when I joined the police. I couldn't think of anything I'd rather be doing in the world at that time. Unfortunately that feeling only lasted a couple of years, but there are many police officers I know who maintained it for their twenty-five-year service.

The reason I call it 'nirvana' category, is that these people are doing what they feel they were born to do in life and are also lucky enough to get paid for it, get paid holidays, sick leave, maternity or paternity leave and a guaranteed income at the end of each month. It is highly unlikely that you fall into this category if you are reading this book. Far more likely you are in the 'employed' category and have a feeling of underachieving at best and absolutely dreading going to work each day at worst.

Self-employed:

Other than the 'distressed' category, this is for me the worst category to put yourself in. I'll explain. If you are self-employed, as 4.25 million people in the UK are, you are working for yourself but without the security and guarantees you have as an employee. I remember opposite the police station was a small sandwich bar called 'The Munch Box'. On match days, for reasons I am sure you can work out, it was a popular 'selfie spot' for female match goers. But it was also popular with the police, being so close to our place of work. The chap who ran the sandwich shop would stand proudly by the till and take the money. Someone else would make the sandwiches for you. And every summer for two weeks the shop would close and a notice would explain that the owners needed a holiday too.

It occurred to me that the owner could quite easily have let the staff he employed making the sandwiches (surely the most important part of the business) - run the shop in his absence. But clearly they could not be trusted to take the actual money and give the change – the role the business owner played. So, instead, for two weeks each year, it closed down and everyone fucked off to Waitrose instead! The lack of income from closing must have doubled the cost of their annual holiday.

Let's imagine you get a job working for a building company and, along with others, you spend forty hours a week for a whole month building an extension to a property. You are proud of the work done and at the end of the month you go to the pub to celebrate over a few beers. But your card is declined as there are not enough funds in your account. You phone up the boss who explains that money is tight and they can't pay you just at the moment. While in theory that *could* happen if you were employed, it happens *all the time* when you are self-employed. Getting paid for your work, chasing invoices and keeping up to date with the books is going to be a constant in your life. Every moment spent doing that is not spent doing the actual work you want to do, in order to get paid.

If you are sick, about to become a parent, want to get a mortgage easily or take some time off to spend with your family, then you will need to have put funds aside to pay yourself while you do so.

If successful and in demand for your service or product, you will need to employ someone else. Suddenly you are a manager, but the person you are managing doesn't have the same interest in your business as you do. It's not their livelihood on the line, they just want the hourly rate you pay them. They can't do the job as well as you and you don't really have the time to explain it to them or give them the six-to-twelve months they need to develop. It becomes all too stressful and you revert back to working for yourself, by yourself.

It can work for some, but for many it turns into a complete nightmare. Better off, therefore, becoming an entrepreneur or a business owner.

Entrepreneur/Business owner/Investor:

I have grouped these together in this category. Unless you are skilled enough, lucky enough or talented enough to fall into one of the categories to follow, this is where I believe you should be aiming to place yourself, if you are not already here.

What is the difference between an entrepreneur and someone who is self-employed? There are many definitions for both, but here is my tuppence worth. An entrepreneur builds a business that is set up to work 100% without them. The outcome is to have a business that you can then sell or receive a passive income from being a shareholder.

To do this you need to have a brilliant team to run the business for you. You need a system for each and every process in the business and a mindset to help you achieve it.

For many in this category, they have also reached the nirvana. They can choose when to work, what areas to spend their money on. Many will continue to invest in, set up or work on businesses even when they don't need to. And they are therefore in the much feted 'nirvana group'. They are doing with their time and money exactly what they want to do.

You cannot count yourself in this category if you could not realistically take six months off, away from your business and for the business to operate just as well (or even better), without you working in it. If that is not the case, then that is where you should be aiming to get to. And it is, for us people born without natural talent, without amazing brains or looks, the most likely way to be able to achieve all the goals you set out in the earlier chapter.

Own brand/Fame:

Being a hugely successful entrepreneur or investor may also put you in this category. And, as long as you protect your own brand, it will certainly help with your existing businesses and future businesses. Think George Foreman or The Kardashians to see what fame can do for a business. This is the category many aspire to. You could be an Instagram influencer and grow an audience from your bedroom. This is why over 100,000 people applied to be on *Love Island* this year. The chance to suddenly promote yourself into the limelight and get marketing and magazine deals.

It does come with its own downside. You may get to the state of fame where you cannot go to the shops on your own, or you pop out without make-up on and appear in the Daily Mail.

Your private life becomes public life. And if you are propelled into the spotlight without having the talent or charisma to back it up, you can quickly and easily drop out completely. For many that is worse than not having been in the spotlight at all and perhaps a contributing factor behind four people associated with *Love Island* having committed suicide.

Expert:

Many experts may also fall into the fame, own brand and entrepreneur category. Sir Elton John is famous, but also an expert at what he does. But you don't have to be famous to be an expert. There will be doctors, artists, engineers who are so creative and talented at what they do that they will be in demand for those skills and can charge pretty much what they like. Tony Robbins is an entrepreneur; he is famous but he is also an expert. He charges one million dollars to coach his clients and he has a long waiting list! And that is because he is the best at what he does. Peter Sage is an outstanding British expert in business and entrepreneurship, charging £10,000 per month for his 1-2-1 coaching. He is both an entrepreneur and expert and has his own brand.

But you may not have heard of Dr Bartolomeo Oliver, the world's leading neurosurgeon? He is not famous, beyond his peers, but is so highly skilled that he is a multi-millionaire. You can book a surgical treatment for Parkinson's at his hospital in Spain for $65,550.

The bottom line is: unless you have huge talent, charisma, expertise, luck or looks, then the best chance you have of meeting all your goals in life is to become an entrepreneur – sorry, a *successful* entrepreneur.

Franchising – the happy middle ground?

Franchising is when you buy into someone else's business and run it as your own. The advantage is it reduces the risk, as you will have an established brand and proven systems to follow. The disadvantage is you will usually need to have a lump sum in order to purchase the franchise and you have to follow the proven systems. You won't see many McDonald's owners selling a McPizza to the late-night crowd, for example.

ActionCOACH is another example of a franchise. And it has allowed the owner, Brad Sugars, to set up branches of ActionCOACH all around the world.

At the lower end of the scale are beauty catalogues, where you sell products such as Avon. The entry is very easy, from as little as £10 to buy the brochures and distribute to your friends and neighbours. The downside is you will have to sell an awful lot of make-up to reach your life goals.

For some, buying a franchise has changed their lives for the better and helped them achieve their goals. But if you genuinely have greater expectations, if you want to radically change your life and the lives of others around you, wouldn't you rather be the one selling your franchise to others?

With a few exceptions, for example politicians, most people will fall into one of the above categories. Which takes us back to the question I posed at the start. *Which level are you on now and which level do you want to be on?*

If you answered 'Entrepreneur' - then you should definitely read on!

'It is never too late to be what you might have been.'

— George Eliot

16

MIKE AND MARY, A CASE STUDY

In case I haven't convinced you yet, we'll take a look at two people: Mike and Mary.

Mike and Mary

Mike has three children and lives with his wife in Epsom, Surrey. He has a well-paid job in the City, in investment banking. He earns an annual income of £80,000 and this puts him in the top 5% of all earners in the UK. Amazing, right? His wife looks after their three young children.

You would expect Mike, being paid more than 95% of the population, to have a fantastic life, wouldn't you? Perhaps his children are privately educated. Maybe two holidays per year and luxury motors to drive around in. But let's look at the reality of Mike's situation.

Mike started from nothing and worked his way up. He is currently renting a three-bedroom semi-detached house in Epsom that costs £2,500 pcm.

Mike's goal is to purchase a four-bedroom house, in or around Epsom, with a garden. He wants this so the children can all have their own bedroom growing up and he can sit on his weekends in the garden, watching them play. That's his dream. Nothing too ambitious. No Ferraris or yachts. He worked out that £700,000 can get him a four-bedroom semi within an easy commute to the children's school and a short cycle to get to the station for him.

Let's take a look at Mike's figures. He earns a whopping £80,000 per year, or £6,666 per month.

Less taxes and NI and 3% pension contribution: £2,182

Monthly Take Home: £4,484

Less Season Ticket: £267

Less Rent: £2,500

Less Council Tax, Utilities. Mobiles and other Bills: £350

Less Food, Pharmacy & Clothing: £600

Less Car Costs & Petrol: £120

Less Kids lunches, school trips and uniforms: £80

Less other expenses: £60

Total Spend pcm: £3,977

Remaining: £505

Mike has spoken with a mortgage advisor and they have found a company that will lend him 5x his salary. So Mike can borrow £80,000 x 5 = £400,000.

To get the four-bedroom semi-detached house that Mike has his heart set on, he would therefore need to save up a deposit of £300,000. Because Mike is prudent, he has already managed to save £25,000 and his parents have said they will gift him a further £25,000.

Based on the above figures, Mike therefore needs to save £250,000 and can put away the £500 each month he does not spend. Mike can afford to buy the house in.… just under forty-two years.

You will note that, in his budget, Mike is not apportioning any money to holidays, trips away, lavish Christmas and birthday presents. His dream of owning his own house within an easy commute of London is never likely to materialise. *And Mike is in the top 5% of earners.*

Let's now take a look at Mary. Mary has also saved £25,000 and been gifted £25,000 by her parents. But she decides to start her own business. Mary has read *Greater Expectations* and has listed her goals. She needs to generate a net worth of at least £5,000,000 to achieve them all.

Mary trained as a doctor but felt she would never be able to achieve her life dreams if she stayed in that role and she was disheartened by the hours and admin required. She did enjoy helping other people, though. Having had the benefit of going to Cambridge herself, she decided to set up her own business helping and training applicants get into Cambridge or Oxford. Using her methodology, training and services, she could increase your chances of success by as much as 40%.

Mary struggled with her business at first and was not sure how to find new clients, especially those from abroad. She took on an ActionCOACH and they helped her devise systems so the business was less reliant on her and also helped expand her offering internationally. Five years after starting, Mary sold her business to a private equity firm for £8,000,000.

Mary is now living the life she wants to on her terms and has set herself even higher and more stretching goals.

Here's the thing: *both of these stories are based on real life situations* – I just changed the names. Even if he wasn't taxed or paid any NI or pension, it would take Mike a hundred years to earn what Mary achieved in five.

The lesson here is, unless you are in the top three categories, the best chance you have of meeting your goals in life and reaching your true potential is to become an entrepreneur.

'Don't ever let somebody tell you, you can't do something, not even me. Alright? Your dream, you gotta protect it. People can't do something themselves, they wanna tell you, you can't do it. If you want something, go get it. Period.'

— Christopher Gardner
in The Pursuit of Happiness

17

THE SIX BUSINESS CATEGORIES

Most business fall into one of the below categories. There may be some exceptions you can think of, and many businesses will cover more than one category. But this breakdown is laid out here to help you work out which *area* you want your business to be in.

Service Industry

People pay you or your business a fee for the service you provide. From a domestic cleaner charging £15 per hour to a C++ specialist programmer charging £800 per day, your business is to sell yours or others' time for money. Mediate UK is in this business area.

Goods Industry

You are buying something at one price and selling at another. The more difficult the end product is to produce, the higher the asking price usually is. So this could be anything from a local shop owner buying Mars Bars at 50p each and selling them at 95p each, or Ford buying different parts to assemble a Mustang and selling it for £45,000.

Two-sided

A two-sided business does not provide a service for a fee or purchase any goods. But, done well, they can be the most successful businesses. Two-sided businesses bring two (or more) sets of people together – usually via an easy-to-use platform – who want to use each other's service or buy goods. Alibaba is one such example, bringing purchasers and buyers together, as are eBay, Tinder, Uber, Airbnb and my own start-up business, YAKKA.

They are notoriously difficult to get up and running, but once a certain point has been reached, they can expand exponentially. Remember: Uber doesn't own any cars or pay any controllers to run a network of taxis. Airbnb doesn't own any properties to rent them out itself. But they are both multibillion-dollar businesses.

Leasing

Leasing is where you purchase something, usually at a high cost, and then rent it out to people. At the lowest end would be the deckchair owner working on the beach, all the way through to the Hilton chain of hotels who rent out space by way of bedrooms. A gym rents out equipment through membership; car hire firms and landlords fall into this category too. Banks and investors also fall into this category. They have access to huge quantities of money, which they lease (lend) out at a profit.

Advertising

Get enough people to one space, whether in person or virtually and you can sell advertising to them. Examples would be ITV, free newspapers ... and two of the most successful companies on the planet: Google and Facebook.

Insurance

This is where you are covering a possible future cost for the client. Think BUPA, car insurance, extended warranties and the like. I had plenty of dealings with this category during my time at FOS, due to the mis-selling of PPI. The margins on such products are very high; some PPI commission was as much as 80% of the monthly fee to the seller. It is possible you may be looking at such an area to start a business, but it would be considered quite specialist.

Many businesses will provide products or services in more than one category.

Think about when you buy a new car (goods). Do you want to buy an extended warranty (insurance)? Bring it back to us for its annual MOT and service at a discount (service). We'll also put a sticker on the back screen showing where you bought the car, without your permission – and it'll be damn near impossible to remove (advertising).

Think about what business areas your business is in, or is going to be in. Then look at each category in more detail:

Service Industry

My second business, Mediate UK, is in this sector. We charge clients approximately £130 per hour to help them reach an agreement. The most difficult part of a service business is how to scale it. Remembering that, as an entrepreneur, you need to be able to be removed from the business for six months without affecting it whatsoever, you will need to develop and devise a system and process for others to deliver your outstanding service on your behalf.

And then you need to think about how this will affect your margins and whether it can, in fact, be scaled. We'll look at two of the easier service industries to get into: domestic cleaning and dog walking.

Domestic Cleaning

You enjoy cleaning and want to earn some money quickly. You charge £12.50 per hour and manage to get yourself ten hours per week. £125, or £542 per month. Excellent. You put up a Facebook page and a very simple website and, with a bit of local marketing and word of mouth, you double it to four hours per day or £1,084 per month. Four hours' cleaning a day is taking its toll on you, but you are in demand so you get someone else to help. You pay them £9 per hour. The business grows and scales, but you find that you now have to charge VAT as your turnover has increased and you have staff not turning up for appointments and not meeting your standards. You have to buy insurance as they have broken some items. Your margins get squeezed so much you are now charging £20 per hour and people are using other, less expensive local cleaners.

The Dog Walker

Julie loves dogs and cannot think of a better job than getting paid to walk them. She has two dogs herself and so she is walking anyway, twice a day. It makes sense to take others with her. She charges £15 per dog per walk. In order to keep track and as per the conditions of her insurance, she can only walk eight dogs at a time. That's six more, plus her own two. 6 x £15, or £90 per walk. But she has to collect and return the dogs to the owners, which takes a little while in addition to the actual walking. She has more enquiries than she can handle herself, but in order to get someone else in, she would need to buy another air-conditioned estate car or van to collect and return the dogs in. She pays Sean £10 per hour to walk the dogs, but the cost of a new van is £25,000. Her profit on each walk is £60. She would need Sean to make 420 walks with 6 dogs per walk in order to break even on the cost of the van.

Her margins do not allow for this and she has to stick with running her own small dog-walking business.

Lesson:

If you are in a service industry, make sure:

- You can scale your business easily and the margins in the service allow for this
- You have written and detailed instructions for each and every process you follow
- You have a system for checking standards are being maintained
- You hire amazing people to carry out the service
- The barriers to entry are high, but not so high that scaling is impossible

Goods Industry

The secret to a goods-based industry is to add value to the product you are selling, or sell a product that is difficult to recreate.

I'll give an example: Pasta vs. Pizza

While you can buy frozen pizzas from the supermarket and cook them in the oven quite easily and for a low cost, to get the real taste of a pizza you need to have freshly prepared dough and a big fuck-off pizza oven.

To cook pasta well, you can buy fresh pasta from the shops, buy fresh pasta sauces and throw in some king prawns and fresh basil and parmesan ... and voilà. A fantastic home-cooked dish.

Recreating a pizza at home is difficult. Recreating pasta – not so much. If you are making a good to sell, you want it to be more pizza and less pasta.

The alternative is to add value. Imagine you are making cookies. They are great cookies. They could be fairly easily made at home, but it's a hassle buying all the ingredients, the total cost of which would be more than buying from you. But if you can also personalise the cookies with messages, funny quotes and even company logos, you can then add an extra level of value and charge more.

Lesson:

If you are looking at being in the goods industry, then you need to be asking yourself what value you are adding to the goods. How easy is it for someone else to replicate? Anyone can buy cheap products from China and sell them at a small profit, undercutting competitors to get the deal. Add value, add customer service and sell something difficult for someone else to reproduce and you stand a much better chance of success. Even with that, it is a very difficult area to do well in. Just watch a few episodes of Dragons' Den to understand why!

Two-sided Industry:

This is without a doubt my favourite industry to work in. You are simply bringing two sets of people together to get a mutually beneficial outcome. Whether matching two people to one another for a date, or bringing a taxi to someone needing a lift, the advantage of this type of business is you can scale it quickly and you don't need to own anything.

To set up a business such as this, you need to look at solving a problem – and preferably one that isn't currently being solved, or not being solved very well. You may need to invest or build up one side first before you can build up the other. Uber, for example, paid drivers to drive around a city before they even had clients to give a lift to. Tinder paid good-looking students to attend parties on campus and persuade interested potential parties to contact them via the app.

Eventually you will get to a tipping point, where you have plenty of users on both sides (think eBay: you are likely to find whatever it is you are searching to buy now, but that wasn't so likely in the first few months of its launch).

You also need to think big and solve a massive problem. If I had not opened my mind to every country and major city in the world, using YAKKA to arrange in person connections, groups and events, I would never have got my brain around the issues of logging on to the app in London and finding the nearest person to connect with was in a coffee shop in Glasgow!

Lesson:

- Solve a common problem
- Get your mindset right
- Think huge

Leasing:

One of the most common forms of 'self-employment' is to own a property of some description and rent it out. It may be that you are renting a room to a lodger, or renting out a second property or holiday home. But, to meet your greater expectations, you will need to scale this and that will involve borrowing money against your properties to lease more and bigger properties to rent out. While tax laws have made it more difficult, it is still possible to do. You may want to go niche and focus on student lettings, for example.

But you need to look at the figures very carefully before you commit to such a business idea. Most items you lease out will not be treated as well as if they were your own. And you will have to ensure they are well maintained. My in-laws had a lovely villa in Florida, but after paying local and national taxes, management fees, advertising costs, electricity bills, pool servicing and maintenance costs, they barely broke even each year.

Lesson:

- Work out the maths carefully
- Check the demand and competition thoroughly before spending any money

Advertising

This is another of my favourite areas in which to start a business. The premise is very simple: get enough people in one area, whether in person or virtually, and sell advertising. Facebook and Google are the absolute masters of this. But, on a smaller scale, you can develop a local free magazine and sell advertising to local businesses. Virgin started off like this when Sir Richard Branson started a music magazine.

YAKKA will sell advertising, enabling our users to download and use the app for free. As do Twitter, ITV, The Evening Standard, most information-giving websites and The Million Dollar Homepage which sold 1,000,000 pixels for $1 each. Unfortunately, while that last example garnered a lot of press interest, it was not something that was able to be repeated or scaled.

If you can build a website and become an authority on an area that is of interest to enough people, you will be able to sell advertising. This can be done through affiliate links, Google AdSense, where Google pays you to advertise on your site, or simply businesses advertising on your site directly.

Lesson:

- Generate something of interest that attracts thousands – or, even better, *millions* of people
- If you are able to generate enough interest, you will be able to sell advertising
- Online is easiest for this

Insurance

I'm not going to say anything more on the subject of insurance businesses at this point, because as I mentioned above it's a highly specialised field – and if that's the business area you've decided on then I'll assume that you've done your homework and found a mentor better equipped to advise on this particular niche!

Needless to say the margins can be incredibly high.

Overview

If I was starting a new business today, I would focus on either a two-sided business or an advertising business. I'll explain why:

My first business was a 'goods business'. At The Scrummery we sold hot dogs, cooked breakfasts and warm lager to rugby fans. On a really good day, I made a profit of £2,000. There were thirteen events throughout the year. This meant I would make £26,000 if everything went according to plan, which it never did. My rent was £23,000. All that work for £3,000 annual salary? It was doomed to fail from the start. Each match day involved a full day of prep – about eight hours – and the day itself started at 6 am and finished at midnight – an eighteen-hour shift (and a particularly tiring and smelly one too). So, 26 hours in total x 13 events = 338 hours. At £3,000 pay per annum, which works out to be £8.87 per hour. Below the minimum wage. I would have been better off had I got a job pulling the beers in one of the stadium bars.

Let's say, instead, I used the knowledge I now have, what would I do instead? I could hire three staff to hand out free product testers and leaflets to passing rugby fans. I would charge businesses £250 per thousand items handed out. Each member of the team would be tasked with handing out one thousand items per event, for which they are paid £20 per hour for three hours work. That's £690 profit per event, multiplied by thirteen = £8,970 profit. And I wouldn't have had to leave the comfort of my home and stink of fried onion, stale beer and bacon fat.

The point I am trying to make is to carefully consider the business industry you want to be in. While there are success stories for all categories, some are far easier and less stressful to succeed in than others.

'If you are working on something that you really care about, you don't have to be pushed. The vision pulls you.'

— Steve Jobs

18

YOUR SIX BUSINESS PILLARS

In Chapter One, we looked at the six pillars upon which to build *yourself* so that you are in the best possible place to start your business, or to help transform it if you currently have one.

This will give you the best possible foundation. In this section, we are going to look at the six pillars on which *your business* needs to be built. Just as with your personal support pillars, you need these to be as strong and wide as possible to give your business the best possible base from which to build.

Let's take a look at them here:

1. Business Idea – what your actual business is.
2. Business Model – how you will sell.
3. Marketing – how you will make people aware of your business.
4. Finances - how you will make money.
5. Your Team – who will make the business work.
6. The Coach/Mentor – who will guide you on the business.

You will notice that the Coach/Mentor pillar is carried through from the personal support pillars and that is because a good coach will support you as the founder and provide advice and guidance on your business itself.

We will look at each pillar in turn.

The Business Idea

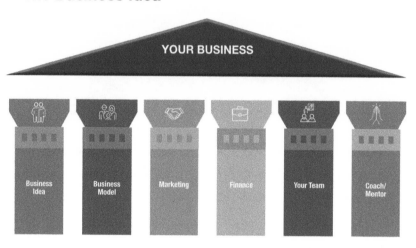

This is *what* you are going to do. What industry you are going to be in. What is the big idea? We have already looked at the advantages and disadvantages of each business industry sector. Which one are you going to choose to operate in? Or maybe you are combining two or more of the sectors? To hone in on the best business for you, you should ask yourself the following questions:

- What am I good at?
- What do I enjoy doing?
- What do I know more about than others?
- What can I do better than others?
- What problem can I solve?

Many people will set up a business based on their work experience to date and there is absolutely nothing wrong with that. But you need to ask yourself, is this a business sector that gets me excited, that will keep me motivated through all the difficult times? Many books on the subject recommend setting up a business from a hobby. For example, if you love making jam, you could set up a business producing an organic jam that is lower in sugar but tastes just as good. But consider whether your love of jam making might be diluted somewhat when you are doing it twelve hours a day and trying to meet sales targets.

I started Mediate UK because I heard it was becoming compulsory for family mediation to at least be considered before an application to court could be made. I knew I could do it better than the highly experienced mediator I had observed for the day. It was an area I had personal experience in from my own life and through my work as a police officer. It is not the business I would choose to start now, with the knowledge I have since gathered, but it is a business I still absolutely love. The reason for that is we get to help people at a difficult time in their lives and help them to prioritise their children. We can't help every couple, but we have 90% success rate and the couples we do help move on with their lives quicker and happier than before. It's a great feeling.

Let's apply the above list to Mediate UK:

What am I good at?

> I'm good at calming people, understanding them and helping people going through personal trauma. I know this from the work I did with victims of serious sexual assault as a police officer.

What do I enjoy?

> I enjoy helping people. It makes me feel good about myself.

What do I know more about than others?

> I know what it is like to go through a divorce and come out the other side happier and healthier.

What can I do better than others?

> I could envisage a national mediation service, providing excellent client service with outstanding business support.

What existing problem can I solve?

> I believed I could help people resolve their financial and parenting issues quicker and more amicably than the existing methods.

The idea for your business does not have to be unique. I struggled with this for a long time, thinking I needed to come up with an idea or product that no one else was doing and this was certainly the case with YAKKA – where you can easily connect with new people, face to face. But it is easier to take an existing idea and simply improve it. Make the process easier, smoother, or make the product better or simpler. Give more benefits than your competitors, give a cast-iron guarantee, or simply make a fantastic offer.

Get to know your chosen business idea inside out and see exactly how your competitors are doing things. Then just do it much better.

While the business idea is, of course, of huge importance to how successful your business will be, the next pillar is even more important.

The Business Model

How you sell your product. Can you achieve a recurring income stream? The Holy Grail of business. Here's one for you. What do Gillette, Epson, Microsoft Xbox and Naked Wines all have in common?

The answer is, other than being hugely successful, multi-million- or -billion-pound businesses, they all have recurring income streams built into their business models. I'll explain.

- *Gillette* – Charge low cost for the razor and make money on the razor blades
- *Epson* – Lose money on the cost of the printer, make it back on the cost of ink cartridges
- *Microsoft Xbox* – Make an even larger loss on the cost of the Xbox. Make it up significantly from game licenses and Xbox subscriptions
- *Naked Wines* – Make no money on introductory offer, sell monthly subscriptions for interesting wines you cannot buy at the local supermarket

All of them involve a repeat subscription. Over time this will enable them to know how long the average lifetime of a customer is, allow them to plan for the future based on realistic forecasts and add huge value to the business if they wished to sell it at a later date.

As another smaller scale example, let's look at the hotel bedding industry. 'Between the Sheets' was a service that sold bedding, towels and other linens to hotels. They had a good supplier, making quality products, but were struggling to sell to the hotels. The larger hotel chains were tied up in long contracts with existing suppliers and the smaller hotels could not afford to purchase the good quality, but relatively more expensive, linen.

The business had all their money tied up in stock and was going to fold.

The idea – good quality hotel linen – was a sound one. But the model needed looking at. They therefore became a hire service for the hotels. Rather than trying to sell thousands of pounds worth of linens to hotels already on tight budgets, they instead offered a rental service.

The hotel would take delivery of a full set of bed sheets, duvet covers, pillowcases, mattress toppers and towels. They would hire all the linen and, once used, would bag it up. Between the Sheets would collect the linen and towels, dropping off clean replacements in the process. The hotel did not have the significant upfront costs, did not have to worry about finding a separate cleaning service themselves and did not have to worry about replacing sheets that were damaged, or towels that were frayed. The business had a far easier proposition to sell, could control their stock better and, most importantly, had plenty of repeat customers giving them more financial certainty and increasing the value of the business significantly.

The same business idea – but completely different models. One model failed, the other worked beyond all expectations. That is why, after the founder themselves, the business model is *the most important thing* to get right.

The Marketing

There are many books on marketing. It is a subject that could not possibly be covered in detail in a book such as this. But there are some important rules and factors to consider when marketing your business.

If you build it, they *won't* (necessarily) come. Just because your business, website, shop or service exists, that does not mean it will attract clients. You will have to market it, one way or another.

1. Marketing is like fishing. You need to know what type of fish you are targeting and then use the right equipment and correct bait.

2. Marketing is not something that should be done when business drops or when you have a few spare minutes in the week. You must have a marketing plan and allocate sufficient time to implement and change it.

Marketing for your business will depend on the type of client you are trying to attract. The key lessons I have learned from marketing – and I have wasted thousands of pounds on incorrect marketing decisions over time – are as follows:

• Work out who your ideal client or clients are and focus all your energy on marketing to them.

• Go niche. Don't try to attract everyone. Indeed the more niche you can go, the better.

Imagine you are searching for help trying to find someone to help you drink less alcohol. You do a Google search for 'alcohol hypnotherapy'. The page loads and you see lots of hypnotherapist services with the following top four search results:

Struggling with alcohol? We will help you drink in moderation.

Does hypnotherapy help with alcohol problems?

5* Hypnotherapy for alcohol and other addictions

Specialists in hypnotherapy for reducing white wine consumption in women

Which is the link the busy mum will click on who, after the stresses of the day and putting the kids to bed, has found herself drinking a bottle of Pinot Grigio most evenings and is worried about it becoming a habit? All the services offer the same thing. But I guarantee that the above client will click on the last link and would even be willing to pay a premium as she will feel the service is offered specifically to meet her needs. If in doubt, go niche.

Of course, the above service may also have a web page aimed at reducing red wine consumption for the busy and stressed businesswomen ... and twenty other niche services. But for each service they will have worked out their preferred client and specifically targeted them.

SEO - Play the long game

With some exceptions, if you are selling a product or service, people will be using Google to try to find you. You have two options on Google. Pay Per Click – which is the advertising at the top and bottom of each search page – and SEO, which is getting your site onto the first page. This is called 'organic traffic'.

It was SEO that helped transform Mediate UK into the nation's largest private family mediation service. I mentioned there are over 200 factors that Google considers, when deciding where to place your website following a search. I strongly recommend, if you are wanting to attract potential clients from a Google search, you focus on just one of these factors: content.

Content can be a blog, a video explainer, an infographic or a tool for clients to use. Ideally you will do a combination of all four. If you are a plumber, you can get more clients clicking on your website by having video explainers of how to fix a toilet block yourself, how to drain a radiator, or how to unblock a sink. You get the idea. This will not only build you up as an authority on all matters plumbing, attracting more clients to your service, it will also mean all those people who have either tried it themselves and still failed, or watched your video and decided it is too difficult to even attempt themselves, will now come to your service to fix their plumbing issue.

One of my proudest moments at Mediate UK was when someone on Mumsnet suggested that another forum user visit Mediate UK to get advice on their divorce as it is 'the best resource for divorce matters'. It probably shouldn't have made me as happy as it did! (The third cartwheel was definitely celebration overload).

The best person to create the content is yourself or someone within in your organisation. You can use an agency to write blogs, but they are less likely to have the in-depth knowledge that you do. I hate my voice, but I still produce three-to-five minute videos explaining a point on divorce or separation and then send them to a chap I use from Fiverr, who edits the video and adds a title, pop-ups and end screen. It then looks far more professional and only costs me £30. One video I produced in this way has had over 30,000 views – a lot for our niche.

Our top-performing organic pages are all blogs, attracting hundreds of thousands of views per year that we could not have captured before. Some of our competitors have started copying our blogs, but thankfully Google recognises this in most cases and we still get the credit for creating the original words.

If you have a tight marketing budget and cannot afford an agency, then Fiverr and Upwork are great places to find help. From logo design to pdfs, infographics, video editing and technical SEO (the stuff that needs to be done on your actual website to make it Google friendly), you can find them all here. Just don't buy backlinks through one of these services. You will waste your money and may be penalised by Google.

If you have a website, take a look at Exposure Ninja. They will do an analysis for free and their YouTube channel has a host of helpful and interesting marketing tips. If you have the budget, they are one of the better digital marketing agencies in the UK. But do shop around and find the best fit for you.

The bottom line on marketing is:

- You will need to do marketing
- You should go niche
- You need to assign time for it

It is a regular and ongoing process. As a business owner you don't need to master it, but to save you wasting thousands of pounds you will need to know about it and where to best spend your money.

Finances

You have probably heard the phrase 'cash is king'. This is because without money your business will implode. You don't *have* to make a profit in your first year – as long as you have planned exactly for this eventuality and have funds in place to cover it. But, in most cases, your sole purpose *should* be to make a profit. Profit is what will help build the value of your business, help you reach your personal goals, give you confidence to scale and grow and allow you to build a nest for unforeseen eventualities (Covid, anyone?).

You need to understand your finances – it is part and parcel of running your business. You don't need to be great at maths, but you need to know what costs you have, what price to charge for your products, what your margin (profit) is on each service or good you sell and how much money you have coming in and going out. You cannot outsource all of this to your accountant. You will be making decisions based on the finances. You need to know and learn them and if you are struggling, hire someone to help you understand. They are too important to ignore.

The Team

This part is going to make or break your business moving forward. The difference between Mediate UK having a disgruntled, unmotivated team member and having a team of enthused employees, all pulling together in the same direction, was palpable. It completely transformed the business.

Leadership

A great team needs a great leader. As the founder it is likely you will be the leader of your team. I certainly wasn't a leader in the first eight years of Mediate UK. But I have grown into the role with the help of my business coach. You need to be yourself, you cannot fake it, but you also need to be the best possible version of yourself and that involves having zero ego and maximum culpability. You need to take the approach that when things go well, it is down to the team; when things go wrong, it is down to you. It is your fault.

Sir Clive Woodward explains this in more detail in his book 'How to Win' and uses the analogy of a window and mirror. When things go well, look through the window and praise everyone else. When things go wrong – and they will on numerous occasions – look in the mirror and blame yourself. Taking 100% responsibility for things that go wrong is freeing and empowering. An employee is stealing from you. Must be their fault, right? You blame the employee. You probably feel let down, angry and disheartened.

It's your fault. You employed them. You set the processes in place that made it possible for them to steal. You did the checks on them. It's your fault and you can learn from this and improve your business accordingly.

Covid came along and suddenly your business was no longer able to operate. Its Covid's fault, right? Or the government's? Or another country's? Wrong again.

It's your fault. Numerous businesses, forced to shut down, found another way to operate and generate an income. Restaurants started offering home deliveries. Mediate UK expanded nationally online. Event organisers created online events.

If you take full responsibility for everything that goes wrong in your business, you will be empowered to change it. You control it. It's on you. If you are blaming others, you will have a team who are worried they will be singled out if they make a mistake and are therefore less likely to take risks or come up with new ideas. <u>You should definitely implement this in your business</u>. If you are constantly blaming others, you will be less likely to expand, more stressed – as it is something you cannot control – and have a poorer company culture. It's a mindset shift that works amazingly well.

When things go well – and if you put into practise the lessons I have given in this book, things are far more likely to go well – then it is the team, <u>not you</u>, who takes the credit. If your business is a success, you and your family will benefit from that success anyway. You really don't need your ego stroked as well. Understand that you would be nothing without the team you have created. Put the praise on them every time and watch your company culture improve and your success soar. This isn't about being disingenuous. The chances are that your team have played a significant part in any success and, even if the success *was* entirely down to you, they have been working on the business to enable you to have that success. Always praise the team.

Recruitment

Whatever level you are recruiting for within your business, you need to get the right people on board. Your job will become so much easier when you do. You need to give new recruits time to settle in, time to understand the company culture and time to learn the job. Trust them to do well and they will eventually do the job better than you can. If they are not going to work out, then regrettably, you need to let them go.

I have had to let three employees go in my time at Mediate UK. Each time I didn't sleep the night before. I felt stressed, bitterly disappointed that I had let them down, and guilty. But it absolutely had to be done. The team is too important to carry anyone.

One of the times, it was a young girl on a government apprenticeship scheme, and she had about a 20% attendance record. She also liked doing recreational drugs in her spare time, so it wasn't a particularly difficult decision. The other two incidents were within their six months probationary period and were just not going to make it. These were far more difficult, but still necessary. First of all – using the mirror and window approach – you have to take full responsibility for the situation. I had hired them, after all. It was all on me. Secondly, you need to make sure you have processes in place so that it does not come as a surprise to them. You need to be giving constant feedback, good or bad, and be completely candid. Thirdly, you need to be honest and direct with them. There is no point offering them false hope.

For all the above three recruits, I had diverted from the recruitment process that I recommend below. Feel free to adapt it as you feel is best for your business, but I have found this to be the best way to get amazing team members for my business.

Put out a job advert. I use Indeed. I also say what the pay is and all the other benefits we offer as an employee. I don't agree with pay 'dependent on experience' or 'apply to find out' job adverts. Be upfront. I invite them to apply with a CV and covering note and I request that they complete one of the Indeed competency tests that are relevant to the position. We mention these three requirements at least three separate times on the job post itself.

For a position in our business support team, we will usually receive over 180 applications. Asking for the above three things – CV, covering note and completed test – immediately takes this down to about ninety applicants. Because half of applicants did not do all three. If they can't read the job description properly, they are probably not going to be right for your business. We then set the test score at a level that we choose and rejected any who fell short of that grade. This takes us down to about sixty applicants.

Following that, we check the sixty CVs and select approximately twenty-five contenders for an online presentation about the role and Mediate UK. Ideally, you would do this presentation in person. The last time we recruited, twelve then registered and after the presentation we invited them to confirm if they were still interested in the job. Ten did so. From the final ten CVs, and monitoring how they had presented themselves and participated in the presentation (did they ask a question, show interest, come across as personable?), we invited three to a 1-2-1 interview.

We interviewed these three people, from the 180 applicants, and settled on Rikki. We requested a reference from her previous employer, which was probably the best reference I have ever read. We offered her the job. Rikki has gone on to become one of the best members of our team, adding huge value with her commitment to the role, her help in building a great company culture and her positivity. She is absolutely perfect for Mediate UK and was deservedly promoted to office manager.

The alternative to this would have been to scroll through 180 CVs ('oh, wow, you can work well individually *and* as part of a team? Amazeballs!') and sit through dozens of 1-2-1 interviews, where we would just have ended up letting more people down afterwards.

You can adapt the process to your own needs. I know a fantastic firm in Yorkshire, called Jason Threadgold Funeral Directors, who ask prospective applicants to leave a voice message and answer questions on the phone, which helps weed out the ones who lack confidence or have a poor phone manner – important in their line of work!

The group presentation, whether online or in person, is a key step in finding the right fit for your team. Always have at least one other person with you, whose only job it is to observe the applicants. I know one company who were going to hire a candidate but declined him as he went out for two cigarette breaks during the one-hour recruitment process. Imagine what he would be like during a full working day? On one of our presentations, we had a lady eating a McDonald's during the presentation. Dogs barking in the background or children screaming are all fine and understandable during an online presentation – most likely coming from my house. Scoffing a Big Mac and fries, not so much.

To help when recruiting, I have put the following in order of importance when looking at who to choose:

1. What their prospective line manager thinks of them
2. Their attendance and behaviour during the presentation
3. Their personality during the interview
4. Their covering letter with the initial application
5. Their timeliness in responding to emails and how they write their emails
6. Their test score on Indeed
7. Their CV

I put CV last, as it is still, of course, an important part of the process. But so many CVs say the same thing, give the same information and, well, some people lie on them too. I give the CV the least weight in the process.

When you do select someone for the role, it is important that you request and receive positive referrals from their previous employer. This should tie in with the employer from their last role on their CV. While most people will give a good referral for someone, even if they are average at the job, if you get a poor reference, a reference that says nothing other than confirming they worked there for a set period of time or, more likely, no response at all – *you should not employ that person.* Full stop. It's a huge red flag. This is the part in the process where I went ahead and employed the members of staff anyway – and then had to let them both go within three months of starting.

For absolute clarity, if their last employer is not willing to write a good reference about your prospective new employee – you cannot hire them. Even if you have already offered them the job pending these references.

Training Staff

If you are a new first-time parent, you will often hear the phrase: 'they don't come with an instruction manual!' Well, your team *will* need such a manual, and you will have to write it. This is going to do a few things:

- Focus your mind on all the processes you have in your head and help make them clearer and better
- Allow the new team member to have a guide they can refer to
- Stop them asking you hundreds of questions. Or worse, asking you once, forgetting the answer and then blagging it, as they feel too embarrassed to ask again
- Add value to your business when you sell it
- Make scaling the business easier and quicker
- Help reduce mistakes and employees doing things the way they want to
- Provide consistency of service to clients
- Stop a reliance on one member of staff being fantastic and then everything turning to rat shit when they leave

For more on this, and the importance of it, take a read of the book *The E-Myth Revisited*. It explains the importance of having a written system for every part of your business in far more detail than I can address here. Writing all your processes down for every part of a role will be time-consuming and can be a frustrating task. You will have to update it every time you make changes (and you will make a lot of changes as you grow) but, you know it already, after all. Doing this task earlier in the life of your business will make your business significantly better later on.

Mediate UK have a fifty-two-page manual for our family mediators. It covers everything from what to do at the end of a mediation session, to what happens if they receive a complaint. It is all documented and updated regularly. We have a similar manual for the head office support team. Alongside these, we have over 300 email templates for every step of the process. All this has taken a lot of work to compile, but it provides consistency of service, allows the team to get through admin tasks more effectively and more efficiently while adding value to the business in multiple ways. You won't need all this on day one. But starting with the end in mind, based on your greater expectations, as captured in your goal setting exercise, you will need these documents in the future. So the sooner you start compiling information on your business into a format that anyone can pick up, read and put into practice, the better.

Coach/Mentor

I have discussed throughout the book the importance of having one of these as you start your business, or start growing your business. You may be lucky enough to know someone with great business acumen or life experience to help mentor you. But, if not, you should look at hiring someone.

A good coach will be the best investment you can make in yourself and your business. But it is an unregulated industry – anyone can call themselves a life coach, business coach or mentor. I fell foul of this in my first attempt at hiring a coach. It crushed my business and almost crushed me in the process. You must undoubtedly do your research, get genuine client referrals and make sure you have a contract that clearly explains what is expected from you both. They should also be a member of body, such as the ICF (International Coaching Federation) or the EMCC (European Mentoring and Coaching Council)

I recommend ActionCOACH as they have a clearly defined system for running a business that works, irrespective of the type of business you operate. They will create a clear outcome planned for you and have worldwide resources to help when needed. I know from attending their various meetups that they have helped thousands of other businesses – each one different. It is a big investment, possibly over £1000 per month for individual coaching, but if I was starting a new business now, it is definitely something I would include in my budget and business plan and I would borrow the money for it, if needs be.

By way of comparison, when I had to go and work at the Financial Ombudsman Service, leaving my family and working just part-time on my business in the evening, I had incurred debts of over £50,000. Had I spent less than half of that on a coach, I would have received two years' worth of individual coaching and, without a doubt, I would not have been in the mess I had found myself in.

My ActionCOACH, Simon Ellson, is a multi-award-winning coach who has helped many other businesses grow. He is not only an excellent coach and mentor, but has become a good friend as well. When I started using ActionCOACH, it was a significant investment for the business. I had to constantly check in with myself that it was an investment I was making and not just another cost. I gambled that it would pay back in time and that has certainly come true.

I went to a training session in Leeds, run by two fantastic speakers: Gavin Ingham and Philip Hesketh. If you get a chance to attend one of their events, or any event they are speaking at, I highly recommend doing so.

Walking into a room of hundreds of salespeople, my anxiety shot through the roof, so I sat on my own at an empty table in the middle of the room. Within a minute of me sitting down, another man came over and sat next to me. He had been sitting with his team – a landscape gardening company – but had seen me on my own and decided to join me. What a nice bloke! We chatted about our businesses and it transpired that he had built up his landscape business to a turnover of £10 million. His secret? He had hired an ActionCOACH and simply put into practice everything he had advised him to do. He hadn't looked back and the business now managed itself while he was setting up another new business.

It is no coincidence that there are thousands of similar success stories, not just in the UK but around the world. You don't have to use ActionCOACH and you should certainly do your own research, but getting a great coach or mentor to help you on your journey is a proven part of making you a great entrepreneur, owning a successful business. You don't have to know it all and do it all yourself.

Did I follow my own advice and get a coach when I started YAKKA, you may ask? Well, no, I was exceedingly fortunate that, on hearing my plans and vision for YAKKA, Simon agreed to join me as a cofounder of the business and wanted to help build it together.

It's amazing having someone with Simon's experience on hand to grow this business into a worldwide app to help connect people and make it easier for people to get out and do more with their time. All this because I hired my first business coach.

'If you talk about it, it's a dream. If you envision it, it's possible. If you schedule it, it's real.'

– Tony Robbins

19

BUSINESS TIPS TO STOP YOU GOING MAD

So, you have now got your six foundation pillars for you in place and you have started assembling the pillars that will support your business, allowing it to grow and provide the life for you and your family that you set out in your goal setting exercise.

What other tips can I share with you? Or, rather, what other mistakes have I made, or seen made, that I want you to avoid? Let's go through them here. I hope they help.

Ignore the dodgy song lyrics

Fairground Attraction sang the song with the lyrics: 'It's got to beeeeeee, perfect'

With respect to Fairground Attraction, no, it doesn't have to be. It has to be *good enough*. If you are waiting for the perfect product to be developed, the perfect piece of software, the perfect service or offering, you will never get started. You need to produce something that is good enough. And then work continually to improve it. What *you* feel is perfect for your clients might be far from it. Get it built, developed or implemented, and get feedback.

When I started Mediate UK (then Surrey Mediation Service), I wanted to offer mediation over the phone, nationally. But when I started offering mediation as a service, people wanted it face-to-face and locally to them. Had I spent five months creating the perfect phone mediation service, invested in marketing, purchased phones and software to allow me to carry out the service, the business would have gone bust before it even had a chance to start. Instead, I was able to offer what clients wanted and then build and develop it from there.

Tip: Just get started. You won't regret it.

Julie Andrews, in the Sound of Music, sang: 'Let's start at the very beginning. A very good place to start.'

Well, with respect, Julie, you and your mellifluous nuns are completely wrong! You want to start at *the end*. Begin with the end in mind. What do you want your business to look like in a few years? What does it *need* to look like to meet your and your partner's goals?

If you were building a house, you wouldn't start throwing a few bricks together and see where you ended up. Many people will know that Jeff Bezos started Amazon as a bookstore. But not many people know that the idea was originally called 'The Everything Store'. He had the vision to use the internet to sell anything and everything, *before* he started selling books. He just chose books to start with as it was something he felt he could do better than the competition, they don't go off and are relatively small to post. The vision was always huge. And he hasn't done too badly since.

When building a property, you have a plan to follow and an idea of whether you are building a single-storey bungalow or a huge tower block. *Clue: aim to build the huge tower block.*

Tip: Start with the end in mind.

Your Business is Your Baby

Are you a parent? Or has someone close to you been a parent? I'll give you a clue – ask your mum or dad! The life cycle of a business is very much like the life cycle of a child.

At the beginning, the baby years, the business is 100% reliant on you. It would literally die without you. The business is you, and you are the business. But you don't want it to be that way always.

The toddler years. As your business grows, you may well experience the 'terrible twos'. The tantrums and stresses. This is the perfect time to get yourself a business coach if you have not done so already. You need to have set rules and processes in place. Just as you need consistency and rules for your toddler.

By the time your business has grown to what we call the 'teenage years', it is starting to look like it can operate without you. Just like you may leave a teenager alone in the house for a night out or even a weekend away, so you should be able to leave your business for a two-week holiday, without it imploding or closing for this time. Or worse, without you ruining the holiday for everyone by checking in every few hours.

Finally, your business becomes an adult. It is able to operate perfectly well without you and you can even start to reap the benefits – your adult child can now collect you from the pub! Your business can start to pay you a dividend without you having to be working in the business for twelve hours per day.

I hope this analogy makes sense. But, with your business, you really want to be aiming to complete this parenting cycle within five years, not having to wait eighteen years as you would with a child. And I am certainly not suggesting you sell your children at the end of raising them. But you must start to let your business run without you. Trust me on this. Done correctly, the people you employ will end up carrying out their roles far better than you. And besides, there is no way you can possibly carry out every role within the business as you grow. So you might as well start planning for it now. Don't be the bottleneck in your own business. Be the guiding parent that allows it to flourish under your loving eyes.

Be more nun – get into the habit

One book you will probably come across on your journey is *Atomic Habits*. I struggled with the book myself, but that doesn't mean the contents are not worth digesting. To become successful, you don't need to get up at 5 am every day, meditate, do something each day that scares you, make five cold calls or anything else like that. But habits do accumulate over time. What you do each day will compound. I have the following suggestions:

Have no more than three items on your daily 'to-do list'. You can usually manage to do three things each day, right? If you have twenty-one things to do, spread them out over a week on seven different to do-lists. One of these tasks must be aimed at improving your business. Whether it is writing a page of your staff manual or compiling information for a blog. It may be recording a 'how to' video, or stalking a competitor. Do just one thing each day that will improve your business. Giving yourself just three things to do per day will allow you to tackle anything else that is thrown at you, leave you time to work on yourself and still allow you to grow your business.

Daily tasks:

1. Do an action that will improve your business. However small.
2. Do an activity that will improve you as a person.
3. Do a task on your to-do list.

If you put both these things into place immediately – and, come on, I am sure you can, no matter how busy you are, then after five years, you will have undertaken 1825 actions to better or improve your business These little habits matter, they compound and they are easily achievable.

Now, let's look at you – another great habit is to put in place just one thing each day that improves you. This may be a thirty-minute walk or run. A trip to the gym. It may be reading a chapter of a business book, an autobiography or a self-help book. Over the next five years – with the exception of a few days, such as Christmas – do not allow yourself to have any 'nothing days'. A 'nothing day' is when you have done nothing to further yourself. It may be as simple as reading a blog on something you find helpful for your life, but do one small task every day and, after those five years, you will have almost 2000 additional ideas, experiences or healthy activities that will have improved you as a human. It is highly likely that is a thousand more than anyone else you know. Imagine that!

If you really put your mind to it, you can complete 2 tasks per day for your business and one task for yourself. As Nike says, 'Just Do It'.

Go against the crowd

Are you doing what everyone else is doing, or are you going against the crowd? Yes, you should certainly emulate, sometimes blatantly copy, and often follow in the footsteps of people who have already been down the road on which you are headed – including your competitors. But you want to be different. You want to build a business that will help you achieve all your goals. You need to be doing things that other people are *not* doing. Whenever I find myself going in the opposite direction to the crowd, doing things that other people are not doing and generally being different, I smile. It's scary, it takes confidence and sometimes it will be the wrong decision. But smile when you are doing it and trust yourself. To be different from the majority of people, you need to act and do things differently.

I took this to the extreme when I gave up drinking alcohol for eight months. I decided that I achieved so much more, got more done, had fewer nothing days (i.e. hangover days) and I ate and felt healthier when I didn't drink. But it was different to what the vast majority of people were doing. I am not saying you have to give up drinking alcohol to succeed. But I want you to think about what actions, what systems, what habits you can put in place that make you different from 95% of the population. Then keep doing it and smile whilst you do so.

Richard Branson doesn't fly the planes

Sir Richard Branson is pretty amazing, right? The Virgin group, of which he is the chairman, has forty businesses in thirty-five countries. He licenses many others and has built and sold many more. One of the most famous brands is the airline Virgin Atlantic. Richard Branson once replied to a question: 'What's the easiest way to become a millionaire?' with 'Become a billionaire and buy an airline.'

But you will notice that Richard Branson doesn't fly the planes. He never has done. He probably knows very little about it. I doubt, if a frightened air stewardess suddenly announced over the tannoy: 'Can anyone on board fly a plane?' that Richard would put his hand up and step up, safely landing the plane on water. But he is fantastic at running a business. Indeed, above running a business, he is fantastic at delegating and finding brilliant people to run his businesses for him.

Every time you find yourself getting too involved working *in* your business, rather than working *on* it, remind yourself, 'Richard Branson doesn't fly the planes.' It might just remind you that he has done rather well from not working in his businesses, but working on them, delegating and trusting others. The sooner you understand that your business will operate better without you, the sooner you can let go, let it flourish and start to attain those life goals and meet your greater expectations.

Can I control this?

As a business owner, or potential business owner, you will probably be a little bit of a control freak. It's OK. We all are, to a certain degree. One of the most important tips I can give you to help run your business and keep your stress levels under control is, when faced with any difficult situation – or indeed any situation at all – to ask yourself just two questions:

1. What outcome do I want from this?
2. What do I need to do to get there?

You will notice I haven't included: 3) What changes do I need other people to make? And for good reason. You cannot control other people. You can only ever truly control yourself.

I learned from my experiences over nine years as a police officer. You will turn up to a domestic incident, involving six people all shouting at each other, all drunk and all wearing string vests, for some reason. As you turn up to the disturbance, they all start shouting at you. You are expected to know – and understand – the years of discord and strife that had led up to the incident that is currently being shouted about at you. You need to ask yourself these two questions:

1. What outcome do I want from this? *I want the disturbance to stop.*
2. What can I do to get there? *I can nick the one who is super-shouty and causing the most distress to everyone.*

Job done. By removing one of the obese and heavily tattooed vested gentlemen from the scene, the others calmed down as they didn't want to also get arrested, and the chap arrested is given plenty of time to sober up and think about his life.

Let's apply this to a business situation I encountered recently.

We had a client who was abusive and angry with members of our team. So much so that he left them feeling shaken and really upset. But he was potentially going to pay us £2,000 for our services.

Let's apply the two questions:

1. What outcome do I want from this? *I want this client to go away and not upset my team again.*
2. What can I do to get there? *I can give him a full refund of fees paid and say we are unable to help him due to how he speaks to our team.*

I couldn't control how he behaved. I couldn't control how my team felt. But I *could* control whether we took him on as a client.

Don't waste your time, energy or stress trying to change others. Explain your side and take charge only of what you can control. I apply this to everything in my life now. It can make you bullet-proof. As I write, the news is full of a forthcoming rise in the energy price cap. People are understandably worried about how they will pay their gas and electric bills this coming winter. But I am not. That's not because we have loads of money – we certainly don't. But I can't control the gas price rises. I can't persuade Russia to withdraw from Ukraine and supply cheap gas to the world again. I certainly can't control anything the gas companies or government do. I get one vote every five years in an election. And that vote on its own changes absolutely nothing.

But I can control a few things. I can control how much energy I use. I can get into the habit of switching off lights when not in use. I can shove a few more jumpers on instead of turning the heating on in October. I can work on my business to reduce costs so I can take more of a dividend, perhaps. I can, when I really put my mind to it, do over fifty things to tackle the issue of the gas and electric price rise. And I control those actions. It's up to me and no one else. Take control of a situation by working out what you can do, to get to where you want to be. Don't spend any time worrying about what others are doing. *You can't control them.*

'Life is 10% what happens to me and 90% of how I react to it.'

— Charles Swindoll

20

THE MAGIC OF AMBITIOUS THINKING

Raise Your Vision

In the police, I was a response driver. This meant I got to respond to emergency calls, with the 'blues and twos' going full pelt. You get a hit of adrenalin when you first do this, but that dissipates over time. However, I defy anyone who does it to say they don't still get a buzz from responding to an emergency call. Contrary to popular belief, the police, or certainly the ones I worked with over ten years, do not just stick them on when late for their refs (food break) or stuck in traffic. You wouldn't last long as a response driver, if you used your blues and twos without being allocated to a response call, or when stopping another vehicle. OK, maybe *once* we tagged onto a call across the borough when our fish and chips were getting cold – but we would have continued had we still been needed at the scene.

On the response course, you get to drive an unmarked police vehicle all around the country. You would practise safe overtaking on national speed limit roads in the countryside, upsetting all the locals, who would then wonder why you were driving at 20 mph through the next village, sticking precisely to the speed limit.

They teach you to press the accelerator in between changing gears, to comment on your surroundings and possible dangers as you drive and to only indicate when there is someone to indicate to. All of these habits get dropped rather quickly on passing the test and being released back to your borough and let loose on the roads of London. But two valuable lessons did stay with me, and do still to this day. The first is to always be able to see the back tyres of the car in front. From a police perspective, this means you will always be able to pull out from a stationary traffic lane in case you need to respond to an emergency. In everyday life, it means that you are less likely to be shunted into the car in front if someone hits you from behind, you can make a U-turn easily if you are stuck in an immovable traffic jam and it provides space if you want to let someone pull out. A good habit to get into. You're welcome.

The other one is to raise your vision. So many drivers blindly follow the car in front, stopping suddenly when they stop and accelerating when they do. Many journeys that we take every day are so entrenched in our minds that we don't tend to remember the journey in any detail. Closed vision is seen by those idiots on the motorway, who will flit from the fast lane to the middle lane because there is a gap there to undertake, and then realise that the middle lane is not actually moving as fast as they hoped and slip back into the fast lane again, in the same position as before, or worse, go for a huge undertake in the slow lane.

They only see the car in front of them and the space to their left or right. If you raise your vision when you are driving, you can foresee which lane you need to be in, start to reduce speed way before the car in front suddenly brakes as they hit traffic, and can allow yourself to turn off a motorway far quicker and later than all the other cars neatly lined up at the exit line one mile before they need to.

During my time in the police, there were many occasions when we had to close off a road. This may have been due to an accident, a mains water pipe leak or a crime scene. One such closure took place on a high street in Havering Borough. A stabbing had taken place outside a local college and, at this stage, not knowing if the victim would survive (they did), we had to close the High Street down as it was a crime scene.

It caused a big disturbance, as you can imagine. I was in charge of the cordon at the bottom of the High Street. I received a call over my radio: 'Idiot on a bike, ignored our cordon, please stop him!'

I saw a gentleman in his fifties cycling fast in my direction. He ducked under the cordon at the top of the crime scene and peddled through the whole area, currently being 'forensicated'. I managed to stop him as he tried to duck under the tape at my end.

'What are you doing?' I asked. 'This is a crime scene; you can't enter here.'

'I'm late for a *very* important chess match and you have no power to stop me!' he angrily replied.

His demeanour changed somewhat when I threatened to arrest him, but I did seize his bike as there could have been blood or DNA evidence on his tyres. He was somewhat apologetic when he returned two months later to collect his bike from the station. He explained that he is so used to making the journey and had not seen the police tape until the last minute and just kept going. This poor chap had certainly not raised his vision. But *you* should, and not just when driving or cycling through a potential murder scene! Honestly, how important can a chess match be, anyway?

So many people restrict themselves in what they believe they can achieve in their lives. Just like in their driving, they never raise their vision above what is directly in front of them. They will look at the next step up at work, but not consider themselves able to do the job right at the top. They will dream one day to pay their mortgage off, but not to re-mortgage and purchase three investment properties instead. They will set up their own business, but not plan for that business to be a world leader.

We restrict what we believe we can do. And we tell ourselves a whole load of lies to help convince ourselves that we are correct.

Limiting Beliefs

'I'm not good enough'

'That's for other people, not me'

'No one gets to the top without treading on some toes'

'I can't afford to do that'

'I'm too old/too young'

'I just don't have the time to do it'

'Money is evil, anyway'

'I tried before and I failed'

'People may laugh at me'

If you have told yourself any of these – or, worse, had someone else tell you them – then you need to raise your vision. Don't be like 95% of drivers. You need to look past the next day, week or year, and envision what you want your life to look like in five years' time. What changes do you need to make now, this instant, to achieve that? The goal setting exercise will help with this, but if you want to make your life substantially better in five years' time, then you need to start making changes today.

Let's break down the above lies and excuses a little for you.

'I'm not good enough'

Probably the most common one. Our bodies are programmed to run away and avert danger. This kept us safe from sabre-toothed tigers, dinosaurs and numerous other dangers that our ancestors had to deal with. Like a woodlouse, we can emotionally curl ourselves up into a ball and make ourselves safe from the outside world. 'I'm not good enough' translates into 'I'm worried I will fail'. Here's the thing. Hardly anyone in the world considers they are good enough. And certainly no one is perfect. You may not be good enough to perform certain tasks in your business or in your life. But I guarantee you, there are people who *are* good enough.

In founding YAKKA, I knew absolutely nothing about tech start-ups. I just had a vision and a plan, and a whole bunch of energy to get it off the ground. But I used the best people I could find to do all the jobs I wasn't 'good enough' to do myself.

Unless you are a complete idiot, and I'm hoping you haven't got this far in the book if you are, then I promise you: You *are* good enough.

'That's for other people, not me'

'The (insert your surname)s don't set up businesses. I wouldn't know where to start. I'll leave that to other people.' If that is you, and you are perfectly happy with your lot in life, then that is a perfectly valid statement. If, for any reason, you are not, and you have aspirations to improve your own life and the lives of your family and friends, then you need to stop thinking other people have some secret to success and that you cannot possibly be successful yourself.

Here's the thing: contrary to a popular book on the subject, there is no 'secret'. There is just a combination of doing things the best way and keeping going when things get tough. There are numerous books on self-help, starting a business, scaling a business and becoming the best version of yourself that you can be. There are seminars, online groups, lectures, Tony Robbins events and TED Talks. Start to work on yourself and you will very soon find that the other people are the ones not progressing with their lives, not moving forwards and stuck in a rut, while you are living the life you want and deserve. So let's flip this one completely. Living a life that doesn't fulfil you? 'That's for other people, not me.'

'No one gets to the top without treading on some toes'

They *do*. This is part of the limiting belief that, to be successful in life or business, you must somehow take advantage of others, or be cruel, uncaring, cut-throat or selfish. Shows like *The Apprentice* or even *Dragons' Den* play on this. The reality is completely different. Many people have become successful because they genuinely care for others: for their employees, their clients and beyond. They understand the importance of giving and the positive effect it can have on the world. You may not like Mark Zuckerberg or Meta/Facebook, but he has donated over three billion dollars to charity. Bill and Melinda Gates have donated $33.4 billion. The rather successful investor, Warren Buffet, has donated over $46 billion. They have all signed The Giving Pledge, a commitment to give away the majority of their wealth either during their lifetime or upon their death.

What most people who get to the top do have, is a laser-like focus on achieving their goals and ambitions in life. To make themselves better. An understanding that giving is all part of that process. You don't need to tread on toes or be cut-throat in your business dealings. Fewer people will want to deal with you if you are like that. You need to be yourself, be kind and be determined. You will fly.

'I can't afford to do that'

You don't always need money to start a business. It *can* be helpful. In some cases, mandatory. But if you have no money to start a business you have two options:

1. Start anyway and bootstrap it.
2. Get the money. Somehow.

Start anyway and bootstrap it.

This was how I started Mediate UK. You may recall I had to mediate my first two clients from the comfort of my living room, as I couldn't afford to rent a meeting room. I put together the website myself with the help of instructions available for free on the internet. I borrowed money on a credit card to undertake a diploma in mediation. My office under the stairs was so small, I had to pull the chair out to get in and then pull it back in to my backside to get to work. If you are setting up a service-style business, just get started. You don't have to wait until you feel you have 'enough money'. You will be waiting a very long time if you do.

As the old Chinese proverb goes, 'The best time to plant a tree was twenty years ago. The second best time is now.' Just get started.

Get the money. Somehow.

If you have a strong enough vision, strong enough belief and a strong enough plan, you will find the money to start your own business. Take a look at the list below – if you put your mind to it you could use one or a combination of these to get the money needed to start.

- *Credit Card*
- *Personal Loan*
- *Start-up loan*
- *Business loan*
- *Overdraft*
- *Borrow from friends and family*
- *Investor capital*
- *Reduce your own costs*
- *Go without*
- *Do more overtime*
- *Get a second income*
- *Sell things you own*
- *Crowdfund*
- *Obtain a grant*

The ones listed in italics are sources I used to get my business started. At The Scrummery, I needed to borrow £1,500 from a friend I worked with in order to buy enough produce to sell for the forthcoming rugby match at Twickenham. He lent it to me, even though it was money saved towards his house deposit. I managed to pay him back within a month. It was a gesture that stopped me from drowning before I even learnt to swim. It gave me a start and, while The Scrummery business did not work out, it taught me many of the lessons I was able to use to help make my later businesses work.

Bottom line is that, if you really want to succeed in your business, you will find a way to get the money you need. And, if you have been turned down ninety-nine times, then great! You are one step closer to finding someone willing to lend you the money. Keep going.

'I'm too old/too young'

The 'too old' belief is one I can relate to. At forty-nine years of age, I am creating a tech start-up, something I would usually associate with computer science graduates in their twenties, wearing hoodies and baseball caps. The classic example used is Colonel Harland Sanders, who founded KFC at the age of sixty-five. He sold the company eight years later for $2million. A lot of money in 1964!

What you do have with age is experience. You can use all the years you have to your advantage. I mentioned earlier in the book that I came up with the idea for Deliveroo a few years before the actual company was launched a few miles up the road. It is, however, a bit disingenuous of me to say that. Because, at that time, I did not have the experience, skills, knowledge or belief to get such an idea off the ground. But at forty-eight, some twelve years older, I am starting a tech business that I believe will transform how we interact socially with one another in the world. Being older can be a bonus.

'I'm too young' … *oh poor you, with your youthful energy and your whole life ahead of you!* Sorry. That was unkind. People love helping younger people get started and going. They want to help you. You have what many older people wish they still had: more time and more energy. There is no such thing as too young. It's a huge advantage and you should make the most of it (before you get 'too old'!). I doubt there is one billionaire in the world over 50, who would not give up all their money to return to being 20 years old again. Youth is a superpower.

The bottom line is that age is not a factor that should be taken into account when starting a business and should definitely not be a concern for you.

'I just don't have the time to do it'

I mentioned Sir Richard Branson earlier. He currently owns forty-six businesses. He has exactly the same amount of time in a day that you have. 'I don't have time' is one of the most common excuses for not starting to achieve the life you want. You need to *make time*.

If you already own a business, a big part of making time is delegating to others. I never could find the time to write this book. So I planned and took myself away for four writing breaks (Bexhill-on-Sea, Nottingham, Cardiff and Marbella, if you must know) to get it completed. I focused on writing during this time, and nothing else. It worked. I could only do this as I had a team working within Mediate UK that could run the business without my day-to-day involvement and Amber running things so well at home. Delegate tasks, free up time and use it to work on you and expanding your current or setting up your new business.

If you are currently employed, then you need to make the time around your job. You may work ten-hour days, need two hours travel time and eight hours' sleep each night. That still leaves four hours per day to work on your new business. Cut down on Netflix, reading the news, social media or whatever else you do that soaks up time. If you put your mind to it, you can find the hours needed to get going. It's too important not to.

Look back on your six pillars of support for you. Who can you ask for help with looking after the children, or for help with other tasks to free up time for you to focus on your new venture?

'Money is evil, anyway'

Money isn't evil. Trying to get money illegally, using others immorally or setting up a business that does more harm than good, is possibly evil. Money itself isn't evil. It gives you more options in life. And it gives you the ability to give back in the most wondrous and life-changing way. Mark Zuckerberg (him again) donated $25 million to fight Ebola in Africa. Pretty much stopping the outbreak in its tracks. Sir Elton John's charity has helped fund a cure for AIDS, saving millions of lives. Money isn't evil. Evil people are evil. Never confuse the two.

'I tried before and I failed'

This is great news, for two reasons. One, it shows you have got started before, so you know you can do it. Secondly, it means you will have already made many mistakes which you can learn from. Some angel investors will only ever invest in someone if they have failed before.

If I see a failure on a CV for a job, it piques my interest. I appreciate the honesty and it shows me they are a bit different to all the other candidates. You didn't just jump in the pool and swim, you didn't climb on your bike and ride without stabilisers and you didn't whoop the arse of your friends on FIFA the first time you played it.

Failing is all part of the journey to get to where you want to be. Embrace it when it happens, learn from it and get better. For example, I just used the phrase 'whoop the arse of your friends' – clearly a mistake. But I will learn from it and never use the phrase again in this book. My apologies.

'People may laugh at me'

Yes, they may. But they may also be jealous of you, secretly long for you to fail, be unsupportive of you, or try to keep you on their level. None of those things are particularly great. So you can simply not associate yourself with any of them. Laugh at yourself, not at others. Focus on what you are doing – working towards your life goals – and don't worry about what others think of you. I promise you: they are not spending nearly as much time concerning themselves with your life as you believe they are. They all have their own shit to deal with. Take control of your goals, your business dreams and your life. And if you get any negatives from friends or family, just tuck it into a pouch marked 'for later use'. And utilise it to inspire you on to greater things. Remember to ditch those 'nagging Nigels' when they come out of the woodwork. Connect with positive people only from now on in.

What is *your* limiting belief? Do you have one not listed here?

I believed I must be a terrible human being to have been rejected by two fathers and my own daughter. I now know that is not the case and I needed a massive injection of cortisone to fully understand it – from someone called Tony Robbins.

'All we have to decide is what to do with the time that is given to us.'

— Gandalf

21

UNLEASH THE POWER WITHIN

Most self-help can be reduced down to three simple strategies:

- Just get started
- Be consistent (habits)
- Ignore negative people

Do these three things and you will find, after time, you are better equipped to handle life and your business.

Let's take a look at each one in turn.

Just get started

A theme throughout this book is to just get your business started. Buy the domain, read the book, schedule in the meeting. It all boils down to taking action. Don't be a learning collector, doing course after course, reading book after book in readiness. Just take action. It will separate you from 90% of the world.

Be consistent (habits)

Humans love a habit. From the cyclist on his way to a chess match, to the driver who can't remember their journey to work as it is so engrained in their mind. From the stressed and depressed business owner who drinks a bottle of wine each night to the successful business owner who gets up each morning, showers and does thirty minutes on the treadmill and reads thirty minutes of a book, before most of the country are awake.

Your habits define the outcome. Consistency is everything. You don't go to the gym once and get a six pack. You don't go on a diet for a week and lose two stone, and you don't get on page one of Google by writing a single blog. Develop amazing habits and perform them consistently over time and you will see rewards far better than you could probably imagine. It's exactly at the point when people classify you as an overnight success, that you realise the many *years* of good habits you have put into yourself and your business have finally started to pay off.

Ignore negative people

We have discussed the nagging Nigels and supportive Sallies already. You really should spend less time worrying what others think and instead try to solve problems for them. Henry Ford famously said, 'If I had asked people what they wanted, they would have said, faster horses.' Focus on your plan, on yourself and on reaching your goals and worry less about what people may think, or what celebrity said what about another celebrity and what is happening in the news. Ignore all the noise and keep moving forwards with your plan. You will thank me later.

I wanted to put all those things into place, and also get rid of my own limiting beliefs. One of the first books I read on my entrepreneur journey was *Awaken the Giant within: How to take control of Your Mental, Emotional, Physical and Financial Destiny* by Tony Robbins. I liked the book and it gave me confidence to move on and leave the police.

Some ten years later, I was packing to travel to San Jose, USA to see the man himself live for his four-day event, Unleash the Power Within (UPW). I was terribly excited. I knew this was going to be the event I needed, to force through change in my life. I also knew I had to justify the cost of attending and the time away from my family by taking huge, positive action afterwards. I was pumped. Just twelve hours before I was due to leave for the airport, the Governor of San Francisco closed the city down due to the Covid pandemic. The event could not go ahead. Never mind, we could transfer to New Jersey in November... also cancelled due to Covid. Instead, Tony Robbins flipped his business model and delivered UPW online, offering all those with tickets free access.

Doing UPW online, in the UK time zone, alone in my spare bedroom, wasn't ideal. But I saw and learnt enough to know that I needed to do this in real life. And, sure enough, in November 2021 I found myself heading to Miami Airport to transform my life at an in-person UPW event.

Tony Robbins is not everyone's cup of tea, but he has made a difference to enough people's lives, including American presidents and A-list celebrities, to give me the confidence that he knows what he is talking about.

For the first time in my life, I was surrounded by like-minded people. People with greater expectations. People desperate to improve themselves, desperate to overcome personal challenges and better their businesses and their relationships. I felt like I was home. On the first day, I lost my coat and bag, which contained my wallet. I had no money and therefore no way to buy food or drink at the event. I had the choice of missing the first day and going to the bank to cancel all my cards and get some emergency funds sent over or I could just go with it. I knew my phone would notify me if my cards were being used. I went for it, took the gamble and finished the first day at 2 am. But here is the kicker. Because people around me heard about my wallet, I did not worry about it in any way. I had instant support from a group of like-minded people, including the bundle of positive energy that is Amanda Cajano, who fed and hydrated me throughout the first day. It was truly humbling.

One attendee even helped me by lending me dollars and paying for various meals and drinks for the whole four-day experience. Just in the belief that I was good to repay it. I vowed to myself that I would repay her kindness, by becoming hugely successful and paying for a whole host of Tony Robbins seminars for her and her family. She was also the first person I talked to about YAKKA and her positive response and encouragement got me started on the YAKKA journey. She was, rather brilliantly, called Hope.

Hope is a realtor from North Carolina; I would recommend anyone looking to buy or sell a property in that area to contact her. I have never seen anyone with such a passion for property, her clients and her family. An amazing lady.

UPW is an introduction into the Tony Robbins world. It worked for me. It may work for you, but do your own research and make your own decision. All I know is that the money I invested into UPW has been repaid back many times over, through the positive changes I have made to Mediate UK and in getting YAKKA started.

UPW is self-help, but self-help on amphetamines! Tony Robbins is a practitioner of NLP – neurolinguistic programming. If you haven't heard of this before, I heartily suggest you look it up and explore it as an option. NLP was developed in the 1970s at the University of California by John

Grinder, a specialist in languages, and Richard Bandler, an information scientist and mathematician. NLP can change unhelpful thoughts, patterns, habits and behaviours. It does so by copying those already successful in what you are trying to achieve and breaking your own links in the brain. You can go from *I'm not good enough to I'm going to succeed* in an instant. And you don't need to undergo months of talking therapy to make the positive change.

I first discovered NLP in 2005, when I gave up smoking. I had a regular twenty-a-day habit for a good fifteen years. My ex-wife was pregnant and I did not want to smoke when we had a baby. I therefore had a strong desire to quit the habit. I read a book called *Allen Carr's Easy Way to Stop Smoking*. While I knew I had to give up smoking for the sake of my baby, I genuinely believed that my life would be far worse when I quit. I couldn't imagine enjoying a drink, finishing a good meal or finishing some in-bed entertainment without having a cigarette afterwards. It was engrained in me. A terrible, unhealthy and expensive habit. But a habit nonetheless.

As you read the book you are encouraged to continue smoking while turning the pages. It is only in the final chapter that you are directed to throw any cigarettes you have away and never smoke again. I had a packet with fifteen cigarettes left in them. Any smoker would know they would quit once they had finished that last packet, right? I remember placing the 15 cigarettes in the wheelie bin and I have never smoked another cigarette since. Indeed, the smell repels me now and I feel sorry for anyone who is still causing so much unnecessary harm to their body, (the last few funerals I attended were all of people who had been regular smokers). But the amazing thing was that reading the book had instantly rewired my brain. Allen Carr was using NLP to change my thoughts. I didn't have to undergo hours of hypnosis, use patches or gum, go cold turkey or buy a vape (which weren't about then, anyway).

After two days of not smoking my body had rid itself of the physical addiction to nicotine. Any cravings or urges after two days are purely mental. They are your brain saying, 'I usually have a cigarette now.' But the book had rewired my brain. And had done so in an instant. I went from smoker to non-smoker, just like that.

I wondered: if I could suddenly change from such an addictive habit, could I use the same techniques to change other things in my life. Could I go from *I'm a failure* to *I'm a success* just as quickly? Could I go from *I must be a terrible person* to *I'm a good and loving person* within a minute of rewiring my thoughts? And could I go from *I have depression* to *I love my life*? UPW taught me techniques to do just that, and I have not looked back since.

I came away from UPW with the confidence to delegate more to my team at Mediate UK and bring forwards our expansion plans. I decided to launch YAKKA, even though I had no technical skills to do so. I had come up with the idea for YAKKA whilst working in Coventry for the Financial Ombudsman and I had done absolutely nothing with the idea for four years! My old limiting beliefs had held me back. I was nervous people would hate the idea, or I would fail as I knew nothing about building a tech start-up.

At UPW, I finally realised that actually, *I'm ok*. People rejecting me from their lives is not necessarily a poor reflection on me – just a choice made by them. I believe it is a wrong choice, they believe otherwise. That's OK. I now take full ownership of how I feel and how I react to things. The warmth shown to me by Hope, Amanda and the other attendees at the event proved to me that I must be OK. I could not thank them enough.

I highly recommend UPW and, if you want to go, but cannot afford it, there are less expensive online seminars too. Also see above paragraphs about finding the money if you really need to.

I use the techniques that I learnt at UPW to deal with any difficult moments I now face. In June 2022, I held an online Zoom meeting for eighty-eight people in eighteen different countries, including my close friends and family, presenting to them my new baby, YAKKA, and asking for their feedback.

It was so far out of my comfort zone. Not because I was worried about presenting online. But because I was setting myself up for mass rejection. I wanted to get all the benefits across clearly, wanted to present my story and my vision clearly and wanted them to love the idea. Two minutes before I was about to go live, I was mentally preparing myself in my mind, focusing on the outcome and then, 'making my move' – a technique to pump adrenaline and confidence into yourself when needed. It worked. We received positive and helpful feedback on YAKKA and I was particularly heartened that many of them were people I did not know from the Tony Robbins forums who had heard my appeal for help and responded.

You can be successful without attending a Tony Robbins event. But, for me, it worked magnificently and I returned again the next year with Danielle from YAKKA, which I know will only make YAKKA a better business. I also paid for my eldest son, Bailey and Belinda, the managing director of Mediate UK to attend in Birmingham this year. The benefits of which are already being seen in both of them.

'People often say that motivation doesn't last. Well, neither does bathing – that's why we recommend it daily.'

— Zig Ziglar

22

DEALING WITH CONFLICT

As you progress on your journey to a better and more fulfilling life, you are likely to come into conflict with people. Just hop onto Twitter or Facebook to see how people react to others they disagree with.

But conflict is quite normal. I made a whole business out of helping people in conflict with Mediate UK. Having helped with over 6,000 clients experiencing conflict and dealing with it many times in my own business and personal life, I can assure you that the easiest way to deal with it is as follows.

It is not finding yourself in conflict that is the issue. That is always going to happen and there is not much you can do about it (other than back down on every occasion, which isn't a great way to lead your life). But you can control your response to the conflict. I highly recommend the following steps:

- Never respond immediately. Your instinctive response will be from the heart, not the head. You need to respond from the head when dealing with matters of conflict.
- You should first of all ask yourself: do I need to get involved in this? For most social media arguments,

the answer is 'no'. I have been involved in heated discussions on Facebook. I'm not going to change anyone's mind. They believe they are right and no amount of evidence will sway them from that opinion. For anything online, the answer is that you probably *don't* need or want to get involved. I suggest the 'want' as let's be honest online trolls are the worst, they're not rational, they're not kind and they cannot be reasoned with.

- If there is an email, post or other matter that can wait for a response … then wait. I suggest a minimum of twenty-four hours to sleep on it before you respond. But I find forty-eight hours is usually how long I need to give a reasoned response from my head and not an emotional one from my heart. Emotions from the heart are great for dealing with loved ones, children and happy occasions. Stay away from that area of your body when dealing with matters of conflict. Find the length of time you need to respond thoughtfully and stick to that time before responding.

- Seeing things from the other person's point of view is a great way to reduce conflict and increase understanding in your life. For example, when Covid hit, we transformed our conservatory into a tiki bar area and added a table that could convert to a pool table, tennis table or dining table. It was a great addition, allowing us to all get together in the house with the kids during lockdown and feel like we were going out, during a time when we were not allowed to. One evening, I witnessed the kids having an argument shortly after we set up the table tennis table. 'I want the blue bat, not the red bat!'" one cried. 'You've got the blue bat, it's in your hand!' the other responded. If you hold a table tennis bat up between two teenagers, one will see it as red and the other will swear blind it is blue. And they are both 100% correct. Whenever you are in conflict with someone else, try to see it from their point of view. As a minimum you will reduce the conflict, at best you may find out they are also correct and you can learn something new.

- Decide on the real outcome you want. In a heated argument with my wife it turned out I was 100% correct and she was completely in the wrong. OK, fair enough, that has never actually happened! But what do you want the outcome to be? If in conflict with someone you care about, the ongoing relationship is probably more important than who is actually correct, or your precious ego. If, through a series of carefully bulleted PowerPoint presentations, Alexa confirmations and Wikipedia references, it turns out you were correct, but your wife is so upset with you still that she doesn't talk to you for three days... have you *really* come out as a winner?

When dealing with clients, friends, family, business associates or anyone else, don't worry when you come into conflict with them. Just ask yourself what you want the outcome to be and relentlessly pursue it. You are unlikely to bring them round to your way of thinking, at best you may reach a compromise – if you can de-escalate the conflict and move forwards, putting your focus back on pursuing your life goals and your greater expectations, then you have a good result.

Dealing correctly with conflict in business or in your relationships is only going to be benefit you. Having run a family mediation and amicable divorce service for twelve years, I wanted to list my recommendations for dealing with conflict with your partner.

1. Take time to respond from the head, and not the heart

2. Separate out emotive issue (they have a new partner) from practical issues (when will the children see their parents?)

3. Focus on the outcome you want (I want to have a hugely successful and fulfilling life)

4. Stay away from revenge tactics (the best revenge you can take is to start living a hugely successful and fulfilling life)

5. Make a plan of what you want your new life to look like in one year's time. And focus all your energy into achieving that plan. Do the goal setting exercise I recommend in this book.

Relationships ending are tough but as discussed in our pillars of support, healthy relationships are key to your success and happiness. You will have read about how poorly I let my relationships affect my own mental health. I took each one as a personal failure and rejection of me as a person. I thought I had lost my reason for being. My source of happiness. None of this, of course, was true.

In a relationship, you want the maths to be wrong. The best relationships are where $1 + 1 = 3$. By being together, you bring out the best in each other, and your sum is larger than your individual parts. A relationship is something you both invest in. You simply need to focus on your positive contribution. If you both focus on your own contribution and not what the other person is contributing, you will know that you have done all you could to make the relationship work.

If your relationship is a 1 + 1 = 2, that's OK. You can continue as you are. But why not work together to make your relationship amazing? Take some time to go through your goal setting exercise together and start to build a better and exciting future, aligned to both your greater expectations. It works.

Finally, you may be in a relationship where 1 + 1 = <2. This is where, together, you make each other less than what you are. This was certainly the case with my first marriage. We just didn't work together and bought out the worst in one another. If you are in such a relationship, you need to make changes and take action to improve it *now*. It is one of your six pillars of support and you will need it if you intend to build the life you dream of.

There are three parts to any relationship. The first part is you. The second part is your partner. The third part is the relationship itself. It's important to differentiate the three. When a relationship breaks down, most people focus on their partner or themselves as the issue. That's not the case. I love cheese. I love chocolate too. But chocolate-covered cheese does not make a great match. It's the outcome of the combined parts that forms the relationship. If you played your part in giving the best you could, when a relationship ends or is ending, you have nothing to feel ashamed or downbeat about. You just need to find the strawberry to your chocolate, or the chutney to your cheese!

Focus on working on *you*. On being the best you can be. And you will attract the person who will help you rise up even further, and vice versa. Find your 1 + 1 = 3.

'Whoever is happy will make others happy too.'

— Anne Frank

23

A WORD ON MENTAL HEALTH

L et's take a moment to close our eyes and count to forty … Go! 1, 2, 3 … come back when you are finished. Are you there? Hello again; someone in the world just killed themselves through suicide.

Every forty seconds someone will take their own life. Imagine how many have done so by the time you have reached this stage in the book? On paper, suicide is the most difficult thing to understand. Why on earth would you take your own life? Why would you do that to your friends, family and children? It just doesn't make any sense. But Marilyn Monroe, Robin Williams, Kurt Cobain, Margot Kidder (Louis Lane) and Caroline Flack – hugely talented people, loved by many – all decided that taking their own life was the only option open to them. According to the World Health Organisation, it is the twelfth leading cause of death in the world. It is a real, tragic and completely preventable event.

Taking time to understand mental health, supporting those you believe to be suffering, making yourself available for anyone to talk to and not dismissing attempts as 'just a cry for help!' (I mean shit, really?) – all of these are essential.

The best way I can describe it and this is just my own feelings at the time, is using an analogy of the film *127 Hours*. The film depicts the true story of a mountain climber who, while canyoneering in Utah, gets trapped by a rock in a deep canyon. *Spoiler alert* … he cuts off his own arm in order to free himself. No one in their right mind would cut their own arm off, right? But for him it made perfect sense. Doing so allowed him to get free and in doing so saved his own life.

I felt very much the same. No one in their right mind would try to kill themselves, right? But the pain in my own brain was so intense, the wires were so jumbled, the cells so scrambled, that stopping that pain seemed a better option than any other options I could think of at that time. Of course, I know that was not the case. And I know I would never put my children, wife or family through such misery, but when you are in the depths of depression you are not thinking clearly. You just want to make the pain stop – *in any way you can.*

I messaged Emma, even though I didn't know her very well. She didn't know at that time, that her positive intervention prevented me from serious injury or death that night in the Travelodge. But I picked Emma as she had always posted on Facebook that she was available to help anyone suffering. It would be great if you did the same on your own social media profiles. You never know when your help may be needed. It may be that someone turns to you because they feel they can't turn to someone else closer to them.

Celebrities such as Tyson Fury, Josh Groban, Bruce Springsteen, Kirsten Dunst, Katy Perry and Dwayne Johnson are among famous people you would think have life pretty much nailed but they have all come out and openly talked about their struggles with depression.

I felt ashamed of mine. Felt people would not want to be associated with me if they knew my 'dirty secret'. When life takes a turn for the worse, as it often does, it could almost kill me. I had no support in place, which is why I now make sure my support pillars are strong. If you are struggling, get help. Be open and honest, or even write it all up in a book like I have done. But never suffer alone.

Negative	Positive
My own father abandoning me	I try and be the best father I can be to my children
My daughter not wanting anything to do with me	I try to become successful in business so I can put my time and money into charities to help mental health in young people
My mother's Alzheimer's	I grew my relationship with my sister even more, we both use each other to replace the emotional hole left by our mum
My real dad being an alcoholic	I now drink alcohol for only a few months each year and have become healthier
My business almost failing	I became a better businessman and leader. I learnt from my mistakes.

My mantra of trying to turn every negative into a positive has helped with this. I highly recommend you do the same.

He probably didn't know it at the time, but when my eldest son sent me the below message, it was without a doubt one of the best moments in my whole life. In that moment, Bailey showed me I had overcome my own issues with my father and turned them into a positive. I am so proud of all my children. But Bailey has had his own struggles and to receive this message just makes me so grateful to have been involved in his life.

….ha ha ha a lot of it has been because of the way you've raised me for the time you've known me, despite our rough patches I couldn't ask for a better dad, you've taught and influenced me with many things, life skills, financial management, how to treat women and just be the best person I can be, can't thank you enough.

I could add to this negative and positive list considerably. But I invite you to make your own list. What negatives have happened to you in your life, and how can you turn them into something positive? Very soon, every time something goes wrong or something bad happens – and we know that it will, no matter how hard you try to protect yourself – you will get into the habit of quickly asking yourself what this experience is trying to teach you and how you can learn and do something positive from it. There is nothing it cannot work for. It's empowering and doesn't half help with your own stress levels and mental health.

Try to make the positive in direct inverse proportion to the negative. The worse something is that has happened to you (my daughter not wanting to see me), the better you need to make the positive (setting up a charity to help all young people with mental health issues).

Many people who have experienced hurt in their life, either through being bullied, having their heart broken, being neglected or abused, or for countless other reasons, will try to protect themselves from experiencing such pain again. It's natural, right? Try touching an iron that you know has not been switched on – you will still hesitate. You will perhaps be timid in touching it with the tip of your finger first, or holding your hand near it to see if it is radiating heat. Very few confidently stride up and place the palm of their hand squarely on the cold iron. It's engrained in your brain. Danger. Until you feel confident enough in your decision.

People build a wall up around them to protect themselves. It's their way of defending themselves from hurt. But it also shuts out a lot of people who can help and contribute to your life.

You cannot go through life isolated. It goes against all natural human inclination and need. You don't need a wall around you. You don't need to protect yourself. You don't need to blame anyone else for what happens in your life. If you take full, genuine, completely honest control and responsibility for yourself – for how you react to things, both good and bad – you don't need a wall.

You don't need to be scared or anxious. You don't need to hate or gossip. You don't need to be down or depressed. You can just choose to be you. Amazing, brilliant you. The version of you that can handle anything and everything that is thrown at you and turn it into a positive.

You become grateful for the good things that happen but, even more brilliantly, you become grateful for the bad things. Because you know they are going to teach you a fantastic lesson. They are going to make you better. They are going to improve you as a person. No one will go through life without suffering hurt or despair at some point. You will never escape it. But you can deal with it differently to most people. You can use it to make you stronger, happier and healthier.

Just ask yourself:

'What is this trying to teach me?'

'What lesson can I learn from this?'

'What can I take from this to make myself even better?'

'What door can I open, now that this one is closed?'

There is no situation, circumstance or event that you cannot build something positive from. Trust yourself to do it. And you can make yourself impervious to pain.

Stop comparing yourself to others

Seeing the lad I sat next to at school had gone on to become a billionaire, acted as the kick I needed to take positive action in my life. But I do not spend one moment trying to compare myself to him. We are completely different people, with different goals in life and different abilities. He may be able to negotiate a property deal to buy seven townhouses and turn them into one (or three to be precise) of the most luxurious properties in London, valued in excess of £250 million, but I'll wager he can't make a 3-egg omelette anywhere near as quickly or perfectly as I can!

One of the biggest secrets to happiness is to stop comparing yourself to anyone else, *other than the person you were this time last year*. That's it. You can learn from others. You can have people you admire and look up to. People you aspire to be like. But never, not even for one moment allow yourself to compare where you are in life with where they are. Instagram is full of people who look like they lead the most amazing lives. Some might. Most probably do not. The kindest thing you can do for yourself is to eradicate any comparisons between the two of you and focus purely on whether you are in a better place emotionally, financially and physically to this time last year. If you are not, you need to take action on one or all of the areas where you have fallen behind. If you answer yes, then you are headed in the right direction. Heading towards achieving your goals. And focusing your brain's attention on what is important. You.

Finally, if you are looking for the biggest contribution you can make to help tackle mental health and reduce suicide rates, it really is very simple:

Be kind to yourself and to everyone you meet. Job done.

'There are three ways to ultimate success: The first way is to be kind. The second way is to be kind. The third way is to be kind.'

— Mister Rogers

24

STAY THE COURSE

As you embark on your new life, as you take steps to better yourself, the lives of your family, friends and, through charitable giving, the lives of those you haven't even met, you will face many personal challenges. The ones you are most likely to come across are challenges on your time, challenges on your money, and guilt. I'll explain.

Imagine you are in London and you wish to journey to Edinburgh. That's the goal. You're walking and you have a plan of where you are going, what you need, and you have visualised arriving in Edinburgh so it is not even a surprise to your brain when you achieve your aim. All good.

But imagine that all along your route you will have people trying to coax you from the path. 'There's a great opportunity in Norwich right now, lots of money to be made there.' *Stick to your original route.* 'Would you like to buy this pair of Nike Air Force 1s? They will help you with your walk?' *No – stick to your budget.* 'Help, my cat is sick, please help.' *No, stick to your plan.*

As you progress in business and life you will have more and more demands on your time and money, and you will feel guilt. You may have missed a school or family event because you were working, you feel awful. Only you can decide how to prioritise your time but I recommend the following as a starting point:

Priority One: You

Priority Two: Your partner

Priority Three: Your children/grandchildren

Priority Four: Your wider family

Priority Five: Your staff/business associates

Priority Seven: Your friends

Priority Six: Your clients

You can change this as you wish for your own situation. But I'll explain why I have listed it in this order. Just as they ask you on the plane to put your own mask on first, before helping others with theirs, in the 'unlikely event of loss of cabin pressure', you need to be the best you can be to help your family, friends, children and business. Many parents put their children at the top. I humbly disagree. Be the person now that you want your children to be when they grow up.

I also put your partner ahead of your children. 'Wow, really? And you running a family mediation service and all, Ali?' I hear you say. But I'm absolutely convinced on this one. Having the right partner in your life, focusing on maintaining a fantastic relationship and finding time for each other, away from the children, will ultimately help your children, more than focusing entirely on them and ignoring your partner or allowing your relationship with them to falter.

My mum stayed with my dad, as she honestly believed it was the best for us children. She waited nineteen years, until I had finished A-levels, before releasing herself from a very unhappy marriage. She did so for good reasons and from a place of love. But instead she showed us what a marriage shouldn't be like. Staying in an unhappy home affected my mental health considerably. It affected my future relationships with women. I genuinely had no idea what a good marriage should look like until I stayed with my friends Ian and Ali, during my own divorce. Quite a few years too late to be taught that lesson.

Instead, showing your children what is good in a relationship and what is unacceptable, teaching them respect between adults, how to deal positively with conflict and what true love looks like – those are the real lessons that will make a huge positive difference to your children's and grandchildren's lives. That is why your partner is higher up the priority list than them.

Our mantra at Mediate UK is 'family must come first.' We will always prioritise family over work. When Ian was invited to go on holiday with his children and grandchildren, because they needed time away and were struggling with some issues, he didn't hesitate in saying yes. He knew that I would 100% agree with the trip, even though it meant him cancelling a few prior work engagements. *Family must always come first.*

I don't remember much about my twenties, let alone my work at Lombard. But one incident did stand out. A fellow worker called Sarah was in floods of tears. Her mum had just sent her a video of her child singing at a school event, and the brilliant young girl had performed the song at the top of her voice with confidence and charisma, wowing the crowd. Sarah could not attend because there were not enough staff on to cover that day. I promised myself that, if I ever became a manager, I would never let an incident like that happen in my business.

Family come first. They are, after all, the reason we are doing this and the support we need to do what you do.

I put clients at the bottom. Surely that is not a great way to run a business? Of course clients are important. Without paying customers you will not last very long in business. But consider the case of Sarah above. How helpful do you think she would have been that afternoon to any clients needing her help? I suggest not very. How much would Ian have got out of the business conference he missed to spend much needed time with his family? Where is his mind going to be if he felt compelled to go to the business event?

Get yourself, your family, your team and those you spend time with in the best possible place and you will be able to offer a far better service to your customers.

However you prioritise your time. Hang in there. Keep going. Use your pillars of support to help you through the difficult times. Staying the course, however tough things get, might be the only reason that your business ends up being a success. You stuck it out when others could not.

'The only one who can tell you "you can't win" is you and you don't have to listen.'

— Jessica Ennis

25

AND THE WINNER IS ...

'**M**ediate UK!'

As I approached the stage with Simon, my business coach, ready to shake the hand of Brad Sugars, the multi-millionaire owner of ActionCOACH, and Clare Balding, TV presenter (and world's nicest person), I was in a state of shock. Having seen the number of entrants to the 'Best Customer Service' category, I had convinced myself we wouldn't even get shortlisted, let alone win the award.

A few months later, we won 'Best response to the Covid crisis' and 'Best customer service' awards at the UK Business Awards. Unbelievably, we then went on to win best overall business at this ceremony, beating the likes of the RAC, Octopus Energy and HSBC in the process.

Mediate UK was now the largest private family mediation and amicable divorce service in the UK. We were operating thirty-six branches nationally, with twenty-six members of our team. We were also the top-rated family mediation service by some margin.

For the first time in my life I was getting recognition for all the work Mediate UK had done. But none of them were my awards. Genuinely. We only received these awards once I started building a team of people committed to help Mediate UK work. Once I armed myself with a good and trusted business coach. Once I made my pillars of support stronger.

You don't get nominated for awards, when you are crying yourself to sleep on the sofa every single Friday evening. When you have drunk a bottle of wine, exhausted from working sixty hours already that week, knowing you will have to work another twenty hours at the weekend, just to keep things afloat. You get no recognition for knowing you aren't spending time with your children or being able to buy them the things they want or need. When your credit cards are declined. When you are getting four hours' sleep at night and your physical and mental health is suffering, you are very unlikely to win anything.

So, please. Follow the tips and advice I have given in this book. I don't want anyone else suffering and making the same mistakes I did. This is what I have learnt about business. I hope you find it helpful. Remember, reading the book is not enough. To succeed you need to take action. One without the other is like owning a fancy car with no fuel in it. Why not start with setting those goals, if you haven't done so already, and instantly become one of the top 30% of people?

A final piece of advice

Never put the responsibility for your happiness onto someone else. It's too important and too big a responsibility. Take full ownership of how you treat yourself, ownership of your future and ownership of your own mental wellbeing. I, one hundred percent promise you, no one is coming to save you. This is all on you.

Take full ownership of your life; not only will you be more able to deal with all that life throws at you, you will also attract people into your life who are more likely to raise you up even further. Be the best you can be. The best version of you.

Allow yourself to love yourself.

Turns out, you see, you're pretty amazing already.

'Don't let yesterday take up too much of today.'

— Will Rogers

26

YAKKA

There was one question that kept me awake at night. How could I take the worst thing that could ever happen to me – my daughter rejecting me from her life at just twelve years of age – and turn it into a positive? What good could I make from this heart-breaking event? What outlet could I pour all my hurt, angst and depression into?

The vision came to me as I was driving home from work.

I will create an event for teenagers struggling with their own mental health. I will hold it annually in the UK and then scale it worldwide. I will invite speakers who have struggled with the same issues themselves; expert counsellors and therapists to give guidance on how to keep going and celebrities and pop stars to encourage the teenagers and make the event an occasion. An event they will look forward to each year, just as I looked forward to my rugby tours to escape.

I will invite 10,000 children and young adults aged twelve to twenty five, with a parent or guardian to join them. It will be by invitation and be completely free. I will then scale it worldwide to help even more young people. And for that I will need some money. A truckload of money. A lot more than I could realistically make through Mediate UK.

It was early December 2017 on a cold Tuesday evening. I was walking across Coventry city centre, which back then was not the most enjoyable of strolls. You would be asked at least five times to 'spare some change, mate' or have someone approach you asking to change up a pound before they just ran off with your money. But I was on a mission! Having spent a few weeks now at the Financial Ombudsman Service, away from my family, I was sick of ordering in pizza or eating takeaways. I didn't fancy buying food to cook in the kitchen, which was always filthy. I craved some form of home cooking and the nearest thing I could think of to this was IKEA's meatballs, fries and gravy.

The wind was cold as I walked head down through the city, avoiding eye contact with anyone around me. I cradled my arms into my coat as I walked, picking up the pace at the thought of the hot meal that awaited me. I arrived at IKEA and took the lift to the top floor. The canteen was not busy and I was able to pick up my tray and head towards the serving area quickly. I collected my dozen meatballs, fries, loganberry sauce and gravy and I grabbed a black coffee on the way to my table. I was sitting by the window so I could look out over the city. They were spending a lot of money doing Coventry up – and they genuinely needed to. It was, in my view, a bit of a depressing dump. I looked up from my balls and scanned the room around me. There was a woman with a young child. A couple of students eating together and five other men, aged between thirty-five and fifty, all eating meatballs on their own. They, along with me, were all busy staring into mobile phones. I wondered what we were all looking at on our phones. The latest football score? How to correctly assemble a Pax wardrobe with sliding doors? Swiping right on Tinder, perhaps?

I thought to myself, *What a shame that there is not an easy way to connect people in this room.* I could have done with a good chat about the football, or having once locked myself in a Pax wardrobe by trying to assemble it, a discussion on the joys of assembling IKEA furniture. Dammit, I would have been happy to help someone decide whether to swipe left or right on Tinder!

I looked, but there was no app that helped you connect in person with anyone for a good chat. A date? Definitely. A hook-up? Possibly. But just for a good conversation? No. Nothing. YAKKA was born out of my own experience and desire for quick and immediate human connection, whilst spending time away from my family. I then did absolutely nothing with the idea for four years. I let my limiting beliefs overtake me. What do I know about a tech start-up? I struggle to log into email. I'm too old to start a tech business. Plus, I was working for the financial ombudsman as my own business was failing. I didn't so much put YAKKA on the back burner as store it in the back of the outside shed, next to the weedkiller and sprinkler we never use.

It was at the Tony Robbins UPW event that I made a commitment to build the app. By this stage, Mediate UK was working well as a business and I was thinking about other ways to achieve my life goals. I knew I could do more with my life, positively impact more people's lives and take every negative that had ever happened to me and turn them into something great... something amazing, even.

On the day before UPW, I was sat in the bar of the hotel, ordering a turkey club sandwich so large I could have taken some of it home with me if it wouldn't have put me over my luggage allowance. I met some amazing people in the bar, all focused on personal growth and most of them business owners. They all had their UPW lanyards on, having just registered for the event. That was the ice breaker that allowed us to start up a conversation.

During the event, I kept focusing on how I could take my daughter, Amelia's rejection of me and make it into a positive. It was difficult. But the event did make me realise that I could found a tech start-up. I knew the importance of getting the right team around me and I knew I could find, inspire and grow the right people to do the work that I didn't have the experience or skills to do. I committed there and then to build YAKKA.

It was in Miami, the day after the event, that I realised how useful the app could be. Miami is a vibrant and colourful city and I didn't want to spend the time in my hotel room on my own. I took myself off for a walk and took in the sounds, sights and smells of this amazing city. Passing one lively bar, I saw a group of people, still wearing their lanyards. That was my icebreaker again. I shared with them that I had also been to UPW and they invited me for a mojito. We shared an evening of laughs, various rum-based cocktails and inspiration. It was a memorable night with some kind and friendly people. One that would never have happened if they had not still been wearing their UPW lanyards. I wanted to build something to replace that. YAKKA would become your permanent lanyard.

At the time of writing, YAKKA has just been launched and we are busy making changes based on our initial user feedback – remember earlier in the book about not launching a perfect product? YAKKA is currently far from perfect, but I know it will be helpful for our users and they will be the ones dictating how it develops.

I am determined for both YAKKA and this book to be successful. Not just for me. Not just for my family and my friends. Not just so I can feel I have achieved something and finally feel like I have a purpose in life. But so that I can, hopefully, make a difference to the world. Help tackle mental health issues. Help other young people going through what I went through and what my beautiful daughter is now suffering with. Then, and only then, I may feel that it has all been worth it.

I'll let you know how it goes in my next book. Or why not download YAKKA and take a look for yourself? It's free to use and helps you connect with others individually or in a group, based on your location, interests and hobbies. The world's first human connection app. You'll also be doing your bit for mental health just by using the app.

Thank you for reading my story. Feel free to reach out and share your experiences with me at www.greaterexpectations.life, or why not connect with me on YAKKA?

'Just keep swimming, swimming, swimming.'

— Dory, Finding Nemo

In Memory of Emma Chamberlain

11th July 1978 – 12th October 2022

'Omg… 32,000 words in? Wow well done…… It would be a pleasure to read your book. What is it about you my darling?. ….. There must be a close secret bursting to get out?..... You know we are connected forever…. No matter that dumb front you put on!....Behind that is an amazing inspiration, desperate to be vulnerable….. Well, I see you mister!... Love you lots…. as you already know, Emma xx'

Emma, I'm sorry you never got to read my book or know that you saved my life by just responding with kindness to my message. I'm sorry I didn't get the opportunity to save yours.

May your light always shine bright.

"Spread love everywhere you go. Let no one ever come to you without leaving happier." -

Mother Teresa

APPENDIX

Suggested Reading

There are a myriad of books on self-help, business, life and mental health. There are some best-sellers that would appear on most people's must-read lists. Some of these books appear below, but as we have established, I am not like most other people, so I have only included the ones that I have found of real benefit to me, helpful and enjoyable to read.

All of them, just like Greater Expectations, require you to take action on what you have read. What's the point otherwise?

Books I found helped and inspired me to take action or feel just better within myself:

Title	Author	Notes
The E-myth revisited	Michael E. Gerber	A *must* read for anyone starting a business. Read this book first!
Sapiens	Yuval Noah Harari	A history of mankind. Puts things into perspective.
How to Get Rich	Felix Dennis	A no-nonsense guide to wealth.
Greenlights	Matthew McConaughey	The actor's autobiography shares his great outlook on life. Audiobook is even better.
Can't Hurt Me	David Goggins	How to overcome anything in your life. I dare you to not feel motivated after reading his story.
Before & Laughter	Jimmy Carr	Autobiography that includes some wonderful insights and life tips from the comedian.
Finding My Virginity	Sir Richard Branson	The sequel to 'Losing my Virginity'. The Virgin story continues and provides inspiration from the world's best entrepreneur.
Shoe Dog	Phil Knight	The amazing story behind Nike. Just read it.
How To Win	Sir Clive Woodward	Business and life tips from the World Cup winning coach.
The Ultimate Jim Rohn Library	Jim Rohn	The first and greatest NLP speaker? His entire collection is available on audible.
Unsexy Business	Jamie Waller	The story of a debt collector building a business against the odds.
Unshakeable	Tony Robbins	Tony Robbins takes what Jim Rohn teaches and multiplies it x100.
Rock Bottom to Rock Star	Ryan Blair	Another 'inspiring; against the odds' story set in the US.
The Inside Track	Peter Sage	Peter was the only civil prisoner in a jail full of criminals. This is his diary.
Be Careful What You Wish For	Simon Jordan	A millionaire in his twenties and chairman of Crystal Palace. A fantastic, honest account.
The Millionaire Fastlane	MJ DeMarco	Inspiring read from the author who started a limo hire company in the US.
Wake Up and Change Your Life	Duncan Bannatyne	His biography, helped me make the move from the police to starting my own business.
The 4-hour work week	Tim Ferriss	The importance of delegating.
Think and Grow Rich	Napoleon Hill	The bible for wealth and mindset.
Don't Lean on Your Excuses	Steve Judge	Inspirational story of a paralympic world champion triathlete. Nice guy too.
Rich Dad, Poor Dad	Robert Kiyosaki	Another fantastic guide to wealth and mindset.
Pulling Profits Out of a Hat	Brad Sugars	A no nonsense guide to increasing profits in your business.
The Diary of a CEO: 33 laws of Business and Life	Steven Bartlett	A great set of principles that apply to all facets of your life.
Easy way to stop smoking	Allen Carr	If you smoke, you should read this and then stop!

Books that people in the know say you should read.

Title	Author
The Art of the Start	Guy Kawasaki
Tools of the Titans	Tim Ferris
7 Habits of Highly Effective People	Stephen R. Covey
The Chimp Paradox	Prof Steve Peters
Atomic Habits	James Clear
How to win friends and influence people	Dale Carnegie
Start With Why	Simon Sinek
Radical Candor	Kim Scott
Steve Jobs	By Walter Isaacson
The Magic of Thinking Big	David Joseph Schwartz
Who moved my cheese?	Dr Spencer Johnson
Awaken the Giant Within	Anthony Robbins

Dear Reader

Thank you for reading my book, Greater Expectations. I hope you enjoyed it and that it has benefited you in some way.

Greater Expectations is aimed at anyone who wants to change their life. I hope that by sharing my experiences, both good and bad, it will help you improve your life and take positive action to make the changes you need.

One of the reasons I wrote this book, was the hope that by sharing my story, it will help people who are currently suffering with their mental health, realise they are not alone and give them the extra confidence they need to pull through.

I have two quick favours to ask to help with this aim.

Please, take 1 minute to leave a 5 star review from wherever you bought this book. Doing so helps with computer algorithms and other stuff I don't understand, meaning more people will hear about the book. It may just help them through a difficult time.

Secondly, let me know if this book has helped you in anyway. I'd love to hear your feedback. You can connect with me at ali@greaterexpectations.life or on YAKKA. I'm on LinkedIn too, just search for alicarter-yakka.

If for any reason, you hated the book, that's ok. But perhaps don't share with me….you will have read how poorly I deal with rejection!

AUTHOR BIO

Ali Carter is a former police officer, chef and father to four children. He founded Mediate UK, the nation's largest private and top-rated family mediation and amicable divorce service. He is founder of YAKKA, an app that helps connect people in real life.

Now a published author, Ali is available for public speaking and can help you or your team set your life and business goals.

Based in Surrey, Ali has a strong desire to help young people with their mental health. He is a support worker and volunteer for a young person's mental health charity.

He is also a keen supporter of mental health charities and the England Rugby Team.

See www.greaterexpectations.life for more information about Ali.

Milton Keynes UK
Ingram Content Group UK Ltd.
UKHW041848101223
434131UK00002B/2